TIBET IN REVOLT

TIBET IN REVOLT

George N. Patterson

FABER AND FABER

24 Russell Square

London

First published in mcmlx
by Faber and Faber Limited
24 Russell Square London W.C.1
Printed in Great Britain by
Latimer Trend & Co Ltd Plymouth

If all men were alike there would be no appointment of rulers;
If all horses were alike there would be no profit.

TIBETAN PROVERB

Contents

Contents

Illustrations

Illustrations

Plates 15 and 16 were photographed
by *Das Studio*, Darjeeling

Introduction

This book is not a history of Tibet, but a record of the events culminating in the nation-wide revolt of the Tibetans against the Chinese. The recent dramatic escape from Lhasa of the Dalai Lama with members of his family and Government, and his flight to India, caught the imagination of the world—it was claimed that there were over two hundred press correspondents gathered at the Indo-Tibetan border to witness his arrival. Despite this interest, however, Tibet's peculiarly isolated geographical position, its inaccessibility, its vast distances, its ambiguous and politically controversial position *vis-à-vis* China and India and, in addition, the aura of mystery and romance which has always surrounded the country, make it difficult for people in other parts of the world to see the recent events there in proper perspective. How did this country, usually believed in the popular mind a land of simple, peaceful, religiously absorbed people come to be united in armed defiance of a monolithic China? How could it resist Communism with more success than had Hungary and maintain a struggle which could involve world peace?

In this book I try to answer these questions, and to present a background against which the recent fighting and possible future activities in Tibet can be understood. I make no attempt at an academic study, but simply seek to present a short, descriptive record of events in some of which I have personally participated or accounts of which I have received from authoritative Tibetan sources. For this reason I have not included footnotes, but I gratefully acknowledge my indebtedness to many noted scholars on the history of Tibet, particularly Sir Charles Bell. Quoted statements

11

from Chinese and Tibetan sources have been retained (apart from very minor corrections) in the English in which they were issued, although these may in places read very oddly to English-speaking readers.

If this book helps to satisfy a little of the widespread desire for knowledge about Tibet it will have accomplished part of its purpose, but my hope is that it may also stimulate sufficient sympathy for this gallant, reckless, likeable people to preserve them from destruction by a ruthless Communist China.

Part One

BACKGROUND TO REVOLT

TIBET AND ITS DISPUTE[

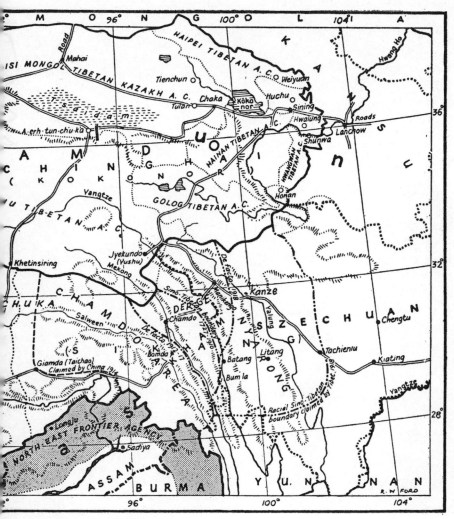

ORDER AREAS

CHAPTER 1

Relations With China

It was the greatest authority on Tibet, the former British Political Officer in Lhasa, Sir Charles Bell, who stated: 'History, unless it centres on religion, does not appeal to the Tibetan mind.'

Not that there are no historical writings in Tibet; on the contrary, there are many, but they are religious chronicles which inadvertently include historical data rather than objective records of actual events. This, linked with Tibet's geographical isolation, its priesthood's aversion to contact with the outside world and possible consequent diminishing of their power should foreign influences enter Tibet, has made it easy for the larger countries surrounding Tibet on the north, east, and west to take decisions involving Tibet, without consultation with Tibetans and according to whatever policy they felt was expedient at the time.

Early writings in the neighbouring countries of India and Nepal are not much better than the Tibetan, for they are of little historical value and, politically, completely unreliable. However, there are many Chinese works, and as these are in the main generally accepted by Western scholars as accurate, the authenticity of Chinese claims in regard to Tibet has—admittedly in a nebulous and even naïve manner—come to be accepted throughout the modern world.

This is not a study of the historical status of Tibet, but a few words on China's historical relations with Tibet will help in clearing up misunderstandings of those Tibetan feelings which finally expressed themselves in raging revolt.

According to Chinese writers, the first record of Chinese contact with Tibetans refers to fighting between the two in 2220 B.C.

when the Emperor Shun drove San-meaou tribesmen into a region called San-wei, which later Chinese scholars identified as constituting three parts of Tibet. However, Western scholars, whatever else they accept, are almost unanimous in dismissing Chinese records of this period as of little or no value.

The first definite contacts between the two peoples was in the Tang dynasty (A.D. 618–907), when about a hundred missions passed between the two countries. These were either simply goodwill missions carrying gifts and compliments, or diplomatic parties making treaties or renewing friendly relations.

The two countries were often at war, for the Tibetans at this time were 'fierce barbarian shepherds', according to one Chinese writer, and sometimes the Chinese were successful and at other times the Tibetans. Ethnographically the boundary at this time extended from near Chengtu in Szechuan to the border of Nepal and Dzo-ji La, twenty-five miles from Srinagar in Kashmir.

In the seventh century Tibet's most famous king, Srongtsen Gompo, extended Tibet's power right into China and Nepal and demanded the tribute of a Chinese and Nepali princess as a wife from each of these countries. At that time the border of Tibet stretched from Lanchow in the east to Nepal in the west and included the whole of Sinkiang in the north as well. By the middle of the eighth century the Chinese were paying to Tibet a yearly tribute of fifty thousand pieces of brocade. When they tried to stop this payment the Tibetans attacked China, occupied Shensi Province and, on the flight of the Emperor, appointed a new Emperor of their own.

A treaty was signed with China. China, when in difficulties with rebellious elements, sent an army to Tibet in A.D. 784 to obtain help and a joint Tibetan and Chinese army recovered Changan, the capital.

It was at this period that Buddhism was introduced into Tibet, first of all through the Chinese and Nepali wives of Srongtsen Gompo and then in the reign of Tihtsong Detsen (A.D. 741) by pundits from India. Towards the end of the ninth century there was a religious revival throughout Tibet and a treaty was signed with China in A.D. 877 dealing with the boundaries then fixed between Tibet and China at Chorten Karpo (the actual White Chorten giving the place its name is still standing). The details of the treaty were engraved in Tibetan and Chinese on three separate pillars, one in Lhasa, another at Sian (Shensi Province) and the third at Chorten Karpo itself.

Although Chinese historical and political influence up to the ninth century was tenuous and fluctuating Chinese cultural influence was extensive and permanent. From being 'fierce barbarian shepherds' with red-painted faces, dressed in felt and skins, the Tibetans gradually absorbed Chinese habits and civilization. The rulers and officials took to wearing brocade and silk, sent their children to Chinese schools to be taught the classics, and invited scholars from China to come to Tibet to compose official reports. Silkworms' eggs, mulberry trees, whisky, barley beer, and cheese were introduced, and tea from China became the national drink. Chinese workmen taught Tibetans how to make writing-brushes; to this day the Tibetans use the wooden or bamboo stylus in the same way as the ancient Chinese did before the invention of the brush. Buddhist scriptures, medical treatises and musical instruments were also sent from China, until by the thirteenth century Tibet, while racially antagonistic to and politically independent of China, was culturally little different from her.

In the thirteenth century Tibet became a vassal state of the all-conquering Mongols under Jenghis Khan. When Phagspa, nephew of the famous Sakya Pandita of the large Sakya monastery, visited Kublai Khan in 1253 he became so popular that he was made Kublai's spiritual guide. Later he was raised to the rank of priest-king of Tibet and constituted the ruler of: (1) Tibet proper, comprising the thirteen districts of Ü and Tsang, (2) Kham and (3) Amdo. From that time Tibet was ruled by the Sakya lamas as a theocracy, for Phagspa had been granted the right to make the succession to the throne hereditary in his family, with his seat in Sakya Dzong in West Tibet.

The early Buddhism had become corrupted by the shamanistic devil-worshipping practices and other licentious activities. These, together with the constant inter-monastery fighting of the lamas or priests, put the Buddhist religion in danger of becoming extinct.

But in the middle of the fourteenth century the great religious reformer, Tsong-ka-pa, was born in north-eastern Tibet. He revived the religion in a purer form, insisted on the celibacy of the priesthood, forbade the drinking of alcohol, and curtailed the proliferation of the demon gods which had invaded the Tibetan religion and the superstitious worship accorded to them. His followers became known as Ge-luk-pas, 'Those on the Way to Virtue', or commonly 'The Yellow Hats' to distinguish them from 'The Red Hats' of his predecessors. For the past three hundred years the Ge-luk-pas have been the most powerful sect in Tibet, and the present Dalai Lama is its head.

Tsong-ka-pa, however, was not the first Dalai Lama. The line of Dalai Lamas did not start until the end of the fourteenth century, and the title of Dalai Lama was not created until the sixteenth century when it was given by the Mongolian king to the third in the line of succession.

The first Dalai Lama had a humble beginning in western Tibet. He was the third son of a herdsman, and was born in an enclosure where the cattle were driven for the night. That night some robbers came, and he was hidden by his mother in a heap of stones. When she returned in the morning she discovered that the baby was still alive and guarded by a crow. This was taken as a sign, that he was destined for some great future, and he became a monk. While still a boy he precociously compiled, on his father's death, a religious book for the remission of his father's sins. He followed this early venture into literature with other books which he claimed were 'free from the three faults of More, Less and Mistake'.

He visited Tsong-ka-pa and received instruction from him, as well as one of his priestly skirts as a weapon of spiritual power. In time he came to be known as 'The Perfector of the Priesthood', and two of the largest monasteries in Tibet were founded by him, including Drepung, damaged in the recent fighting in Lhasa. He was High Priest of Drepung Monastery when he died in a blaze of glory.

Some years afterwards it began to be propagated that his spirit had passed into another priest who, it was claimed, should therefore be his successor in this monastery. This was the first time that such a suggestion had been put forward. While the Tibetans were used to the idea of people moving up and down the spiritual scale according to the merits and demerits of their past lives, or even, by reason of their extreme holiness, passing into Buddhahood and returning no more, it was for them an innovation that one should waive his right to Buddhahood and return to earth to help others still struggling on the upward path. The claimant's spiritual authority was increased tremendously, but at the time there was no attempt to extend his authority into the secular sphere.

In the sixteenth century the third in the line was very friendly with the Mongol king. Leading Mongols and then the whole country were converted to Buddhism, and he was given the title 'Dalai Lama' or 'All-Embracing Priest', a title continued by his successors although never used by the Tibetans, who refer to the Dalai Lama as 'Kun-dun', or 'Gyau Rimpoche'.

The fifth Dalai Lama, or 'The Great Fifth' as he is known in Tibet, was a remarkable personality. He had all the spiritual pre-eminence of his predecessors, but his restless and forceful character carried him into the secular field as well. He persuaded a powerful Mongol chief to espouse his cause. This chief invaded Tibet, defeated the petty chiefs and the king of Tsang in West Tibet, and gave the sovereignty of the whole of Tibet to the Great Fifth in 1641. Under him the spiritual and secular authority of the Dalai Lama was securely established, and every Dalai Lama since has sought to maintain it.

The office of Panchen Lama was created by the fifth Dalai Lama. He had a tutor, the abbot of the great Tashi-Lhunpo Monastery, whom he much revered. Because of his deep love and respect he made him the second Incarnate Lama of Tibet, gave him Tashi-Lhunpo, founded by the first Dalai Lama, as his monastery, and named him 'The Precious Great Sage', or Pan-chen Rimpoche, declaring him to be an Incarnation of the Celestial Buddha, 'Boundless Light', whose spiritual son, Chen-re-zi was incarnate in the Dalai Lama himself. Thus while second in rank and precedence, he was automatically the Dalai Lama's spiritual superior in Tibetan theology, a situation that was to provoke endless religious squabbles and political conflicts in subsequent Tibetan history.

When The Great Fifth visited Peking at the request of the Manchurian Emperor Shih-tsu in 1652 he was treated with profound respect and courtesy, and it is recorded that the Emperor would have met him at the frontier had he not been dissuaded by his ministers. Sir Charles Bell writes of the visit: 'The fifth Dalai Lama, when visiting Peking in 1652, came there as an independent monarch, being at that time neither under China nor under any other nation.' W. W. Rockhill, another authority on Tibet, writing of the same period, records: 'At this period of China's relations with Tibet, the temporal power of the Lama, backed by the arms of Gushi Khan and the devotion of all Mongolia, was not a thing for the emperor of China to question.'

During the latter part of his reign The Great Fifth had transferred the actual administration of the country to his favourite and very able Chief Minister, who kept the news of his death secret for nine years by claiming that The Great Fifth was in religious meditation in the Potala, the huge palace which he had built dominating the city of Lhasa.

In the meantime the new incarnation, the Sixth Dalai Lama, had been disastrously sampling the pleasures of the world instead of applying himself to the strict regimen of religious instruction which would have been his lot in more normal circumstances. He was a youth of intelligence, taste and humour, and although he indulged in wine and women to excess, he also introduced elegance and beauty into the formerly strict monastic architecture of the Potala. He built a temple to the Serpent Gods that is considered to be one of the five loveliest buildings of Lhasa and, in addition, composed love songs that are still classics. He, too, like his predecessor, was invited to Peking, but died—some claim he was murdered—on the way.

There was considerable intrigue following his death, some even disputing whether the romantic Sixth was a rightful Dalai Lama in view of his behaviour. When a successor was finally put forward by the Panchen Lama in collaboration with the commander of the Lhasa garrison, the Mongolian and Kokonor tribes refused to recognize the new occupant and nominated a child who had been born in Litang, in Kham, as the true incarnation of the Sixth Dalai Lama.

The dispute rapidly developed and when the Chinese Emperor ordered the new claimant to be removed to Sining the Mongolian Khan replied by sending his crack army of four thousand men to invade Tibet, claiming he was going to place the true incarnation on the throne.

The invasion was successful. The Dzungarian Mongols swept across Tibet, captured Lhasa, imprisoned the other claimant sponsored by China, and set up their régime. The sudden and complete success of the Mongol invasion created a situation that looked ominous for China, for Tibetan Buddhism under the First Dalai Lama had extended and entrenched itself from Ladakh to Manchuria and it was within the bounds of possibility that a new Mongol Empire would arise in Asia.

CHAPTER 2

Chinese Suzerainty over Tibet

There was consternation in China at this sudden turn of events. The Emperor hastily sent an armed force to the help of the Tibetans but it was annihilated by the Mongols after a resistance of little over a month. This defeat discouraged the Chinese for a time but three years later the Emperor sent one army from Kokonor in the north, one from Tachienlu in the south, and then a third through Urumchi. After a series of victories the Chinese troops from Tachienlu (modern Kangting) entered Lhasa, and installed the new Seventh Dalai Lama.

China's claim to suzerainty over Tibet appears to date from this invasion. On this occasion a Manchu Resident, with a garrison force of three thousand Chinese troops, was left behind and communication with China was kept open by stationing small detachments of troops along the Lhasa-Chamdo-Batang-Tachienlu road. The new boundary between China and Tibet was demarcated by a pillar, erected in 1727, on the Bum La, a small pass two-and-a-half days south-west of Batang. The country to the west of this point was handed over to the rule of the Dalai Lama under the suzerainty of the Manchu Emperor, while the Tibetan chiefs of the states and tribes in the provinces of Kham and Amdo to the east of it were given the status of semi-independent feudatories of China with Batang and Litang being placed under the administration of Szechuan. This loose arrangement lasted for nearly two centuries, until the later Chinese conquest initiated in 1905 as the result of the British advance on Lhasa in the preceding year.

George Bogle, in his general report of conditions obtaining in Tibet at this period, wrote: 'The Emperor of China is acknowledged as sovereign of the country; the appointment to the first offices in the State is made by his order, and in all measures of consequence reference is first had to the Court of Peking, but the internal government is committed to the natives. The Chinese in general are committed to the capital, no tribute is exacted, and the people of Tibet, except Lhasa, hardly feel the weight of a foreign yoke.'

In 1790 the Gurkhas of Nepal invaded Tibet. The Chinese Resident moved the Panchen Lama to safety in eastern Tibet, and even suggested that the Dalai Lama be moved to Sining. In the meantime Tibetan morale had been shattered by the priests of Tashi-Lhunpo announcing that the goddess had revealed non-resistance to the invaders. The Gurkhas easily captured Shigatse and looted Tashi-Lhunpo, and were soon in control of the whole of western Tibet. However, the Chinese Government had by this time heard of what was happening; they immediately despatched an army to Tibet which defeated the Gurkhas and advanced to within one day's march of Kathmandu, the capital of Nepal.

The ruler of Nepal, fearing that the seat of government would be lost and that Sikkim and Bhutan might take the opportunity to avenge former invasions, hastily signed a humiliating peace treaty, agreeing to restore all the plunder taken and to send a tribute mission to Peking every five years. An inscribed stone pillar was erected in Lhasa to commemorate the conquest.

Again the Manchus decided to consolidate their position and strengthen their hold over their newly-acquired territory on the Indian border. They appointed two Ambans, or Resident Representatives, with the rank of governor-general, in Lhasa and Shigatse, on a footing of equality with the Dalai and Panchen Lamas. Tibetan officials, both lay and ecclesiastical, were ordered to submit to the Resident's decision in all questions of importance. Even the Dalai and Panchen Lamas were no longer permitted to memorialize the throne but were authorized only to 'report to the Residents and ask their orders'. A regular indigenous army of three thousand men was established under imperial command and given regular pay, and in addition a thousand Mongolians and a thousand Chinese troops were stationed in Tibet.

A general reform of the administration was begun and carried out by the Residents. The treasuries were placed under their control, they regulated the pay of both lay and ecclesiastical officials, they introduced a new currency bearing the title of the Emperor, and they even defined the duties and appointment of each official. All communications with neighbouring states such as Nepal, Bhutan and Sikkim had to be conducted through the Residents, and any entry into or departure from Tibetan territory had first to be approved by them.

This absolute control by the Chinese Residents was not maintained for very long, however. When the Anglo-Chinese, or Opium War broke out in 1840 the Chinese positions became so weakened that more Tibetan troops were recruited and better weapons given to them.

China's position continued to deteriorate and after the T'aip'ing rebellion, when China had been defeated by the combined armies of England and France, she was in no position to take further interest in Tibet.

In 1860 the Tibetans of Nyarong, in Kham, East Tibet, under the leadership of an ambitious and warlike chief called Gombu Namgyal, invaded and conquered the neighbouring states. The whole of East Tibet was involved in the fighting and all traffic between China and Tibet ceased for the next few years.

The chiefs and the peoples of Derge and the five Hor States south of Kanze, in Kham, appealed to both the Chinese and Tibetan governments for help against the Nyarong invaders. The former, preoccupied with the T'aip'ing rebellion and their troubles with foreign countries, were unable to take any action toward restoring order in the Tibetan States under their assumed nominal protection, but the Dalai Lama responded to the appeals of the Chiefs by sending a Tibetan army into Kham in 1863, by whom the disturbances were suppressed and Gombu Namgyal and his family put to death.

The administration of Nyarong was then formally taken over by the Lhasa Government, which appointed a High Commissioner named Punrab (known in Tibetan as the Nyarong Chichyab), to govern the country and also to supervise the affairs of Derge and the five Hor States which had been restored to independence under their own native kings.

The Tibetan claim to the reconquered territory dates from this time (1865) when the Chinese Imperial Court confirmed the claim. It is said that the Tibetan Government offered at the time to give up the country to the Chinese in return for a sum of money as indemnity for the cost of the military operations, but the Peking Government were apparently unwilling to accept the responsibility of administering the States and formally handed them over to the rule of the Dalai Lama, in whose hands they remained until forcibly annexed by the Chinese under Chao Erh-feng in 1911.

In the meantime, on her western border, Tibet was having trouble with the British in India. In a series of military campaigns Britain had either signed agreements for obtaining strips of territory or had annexed them outright in Nepal, Sikkim and Assam. These events in states bordering Tibet caused concern amongst the Tibetan officials who were linked to them by religious and political ties, and who saw in the British advance a fresh menace to the newly-acquired Tibetan independence. Even Ashley Eden, the British Envoy and Special Commissioner to Sikkim, acknowledged in his despatch to the Secretary of the Government of Bengal, dated April 8, 1861, that 'Nepal is tributary to China, Tibet is tributary to China, and Sikkim and Bhutan are tributary to Tibet'.

The Tibetans accordingly persuaded the Sikkim ruler (who was a Tibetan anyway and scarcely more than an official of the Tibetan Government) to return to Tibet in violation of his agreement with the British to remain in Sikkim for nine months of the year. Then the Tibetan army crossed into Sikkim and built a fort to block the latter's communication with India.

There was sporadic fighting between the British and Tibetans on the border for the next few years until the Chinese, fearing that if the matter continued in abeyance without settlement it might result in future trouble, signed an agreement on March 17, 1890, in India. This treaty sanctioned British control over the internal administration and foreign relations of Sikkim, and stipulated that the water parting of the Teesta River should form the boundary between Sikkim and Tibet. The Tibetans disputed the demarcating pillars which the British Representative put up. The Viceroy of India, Lord Elgin, conceded that the Tibetans had 'a reasonable claim'. On the other hand, the Chinese, while sincerely desiring to see the Convention carried out, had no means of making the Tibetans agree.

In these circumstances Lord Curzon formulated a new policy— 'to cover not merely the small question of Sikkim frontier, but the entire question of our (British) future relations, commercial or otherwise, with Tibet'. But it was easier said than done, for no one would take the Viceroy's letter to the Dalai Lama, and when finally one agent did, it was returned with the seals intact.

When all these attempts failed, Lord Curzon, in February 1902, claimed that it was 'the most extraordinary anachronism of the twentieth century that there should exist within less than three hundred miles of the border of British India a State and a Government with whom political relations do not so much as exist, and with whom it is impossible to exchange a written communication'. A year later, on January 8, 1903, he wrote to the Secretary of State for India: 'Chinese suzerainty over Tibet is a constitutional fiction—a political affectation which has only been maintained because of its convenience to both parties.'

During this exchange there were also sharp words about Russia's interest in Tibet, and Sir Charles Bell, in *Tibet Past and Present*, writes of the growing influence of Dorjieff, a Russian Mongol who had worked himself into a position of close confidence to the Dalai Lama: 'Things were happening behind the barrier north of the great palace, and Tibet's neighbours were becoming uneasy. The British Government believed that Russia was making a secret treaty to help China against those who were pressing her from different directions. Russia was to receive Tibet in return for her services. Nepal and other States on the northern frontier of India were alarmed at the news. Accordingly the Government of India despatched a political mission under Colonel (later Sir Francis) Younghusband to put relations with Tibet on a satisfactory footing. . . . At length the mission became changed into a military expedition.'

Eventually the British troops reached Lhasa, and the Dalai Lama fled to Mongolia. He left his seal with a trusted priest and in September 1904 Younghusband negotiated the treaty that laid the foundation of all Britain's subsequent dealings with Tibet. Its main terms were that the Tibetan Government agreed to recognize the British protectorate over Sikkim, to promote trade between India and three trade marts in Tibet, and to prevent other foreigners exercising influence in Tibet.

However, in his address at the close of the treaty-signing ceremony Colonel Younghusband said that 'the British Government fully recognized the suzerainty of the Chinese Government', and that the British 'had not the least desire to supplant China in the suzerainty of Tibet'.

The Chinese Resident replied by recommending to the Emperor that the Dalai Lama be denounced and that the Panchen Lama be summoned to Lhasa with a view to making him the head of the whole Tibetan religious community. The Tibetans were angry and maintained that no Panchen had ever acted as regent instead of a Dalai Lama—'not even for a single hour'. This is an important point to bear in mind when we see the Chinese Communists of the present day attempting the same move.

Negotiations were opened soon after to secure the adhesion of the Peking Government to the Anglo-Tibetan Convention. The Chinese Government at first tried to revive their claim to be the sole medium of communication between the Government of India and the Tibetans and to replace the Anglo-Tibetan Treaty by a new Agreement, but eventually they were persuaded to accept the Lhasa Convention, which was signed at Peking in April 1906. The terms were officially given as follows:

'It secures the adhesion of China to the Convention established with Tibet in 1904. It does not alter the arrangement arrived at under the Convention of Tibet as confirmed by the Government of India. It contains an engagement on our part not to encroach on Tibetan territory nor to interfere in the Government of Tibet, the Government of China undertaking on their part not to allow any foreign state to interfere in the government or internal administration of Tibet.'

Chinese Suzerainty over Tibet

By signing the Adhesion Agreement China's rapidly weakening position in Tibet was saved. The Chinese were not slow to take advantage of the situation and, Britain having denied herself the right to keep close watch on Tibet, the Chinese insinuated themselves once more into a position of influence. The Tibetans gradually were led to believe that though Peking had not had time to send an army at the time of the British invasion of Tibet it was fear of Chinese displeasure which had caused them to withdraw, and that China had since compelled Britain to sign another Agreement cancelling the Lhasa Convention and acknowledging the right of the Chinese to control Tibet.

At the same time the Chinese created a new post of Imperial Resident at Chamdo, in Kham, with instructions to curtail gradually the power of the native rulers and lamas and bring the country under the direct control of the Chinese Government.

In April 1905 the Tibetans of Kham Province in East Tibet, known as Khambas, and the lamas of the great Batang monastery rose in open revolt and attacked the Chinese. Even the foreign missionaries who claimed protection under Treaty rights from Chinese officials were killed because they were identified with the Chinese in their policies.

These events in Batang were a signal for a general rising of all the big monasteries on the borders of south-west Szechuan and north-west Yunnan and the isolated Chinese garrisons were overwhelmed and massacred. The Chinese Government then sent a General Chao Erh-feng to put down the rebellion and his harsh measures and merciless practices earned him the name of 'Butcher' Chao amongst the Tibetans.

Having subjugated Kham Province by 1906, Chao made Batang, the former capital of Kham, his headquarters. Kham had prior to this been ruled by two native Chiefs and the head of the Batang monastery, the Chinese officials stationed there being merely charged with the forwarding of the mails and supplies between China and Tibet and exercising no authority over the Tibetan population. Chao abolished the office of native Chiefs and put a Chinese magistrate in their place, introduced new laws and deprived the lamas of their temporal authority.

For his work in Tibet, Chao was raised to the newly-created post of Frontier Commissioner. He was thus placed in independent control of a vast tract of country extending from the borders of Kansu and the Kokonor in the north to those of Yunnan, Burma and Assam in the south, and from Tachienlu in the east to the confines of Central Tibet, near Lhasa, in the west.

In March 1908 the Chinese issued two Imperial Edicts, one appointing Chao Erh-fang to be Imperial Commissioner for Tibet, and the second appointing his brother to be Viceroy of Szechuan. These two appointments resulted in the complete subjugation of Tibet for a brief period to Chinese rule.

Towards the end of 1909 Chao had several thousands of Chinese troops in Kham and was making preparations to march on Lhasa. The Kham Tibetans petitioned the Lhasa Government for permission to oppose the Chinese but the Lhasa officials, reluctant to take up arms against their powerful neighbours, refused and sought to negotiate with the Resident. He temporized and assured the Tibetans that Chao would not advance further.

The Tibetans in desperation sent telegraphic appeals through India to the foreign powers of Europe and the Chinese Government, but to no effect, and Chao marched into Lhasa on February 12, 1910. The Dalai Lama made a dramatic last-minute escape to India within sight of the Chinese advance guard.

Thus for the third time in the history of the two countries a Chinese army marched into Tibet's sacred city.

CHAPTER 3

Racial Antagonism to China

It is difficult to generalize about the country of Tibet or its people; and this is the reason why so many apparently contradictory books have been written. Those whose contacts with the Tibetans have been restricted to West or Central Tibet and who have assumed that what they have seen and noted must be true of the nation as a whole have in all sincerity committed themselves to as great a delusion as anyone in the Middle Ages who might have assumed that the races in Europe were similar because they occupied the same land mass.

In point of fact, the differences between the peoples of Tibet are greater than existed in Europe in the Middle Ages, for apart from the great East-West caravan trail there was practically no contact between the inhabitants of one valley and another. The Tibetans have a proverb based on this extreme isolation:

> *To every valley its own dialect;*
> *To every lama his own doctrine.*

I have seen Pangdatshang, the leader of the Khambas, using three and four interpreters while speaking to some of the nomads from the more inaccessible parts of Kham. I have passed through valleys in South Tibet where people from one valley could not converse with those from the next valley except through the guide or some trader who had passed on occasion between them.

Unless one has visited Tibet it is impossible to imagine its vastness. The highest land mass in the world, its valleys are higher than the summits of many mountains in Europe, Canada or the Americas. Three-quarters of Tibet is over fifteen thousand feet in

1. The author in Kalimpong

2. A typical Tibetan village at an altitude of 18,000 feet

height. The whole country is twenty times the size of England, or about one-third of the United States. It stretches from the mighty mountain ranges of the Himalayas on the east to the Amne Machin and Minya Konka ranges on the west; from the Altyn Tagh on the north to the Himalayan foot-hills in the south. Five of the world's largest rivers have their sources in this tremendous watershed, pouring into India, Burma and China their millions of tons of mountain water.

In the north the great Chang-tang, or Northern Plain, is a region of barren plateaux swept by gales and snow blizzards, treacherous with swamps, and only sparsely inhabited by wandering tribes of fierce nomads. Even Tibetans know very little of what goes on in this area of Tibet.

In the west the highest mountain ranges in the world alternate with empty barren plateaux, but with more settled village life and pasture than in the empty frozen north. Trade marts and places of pilgrimage draw traders and pilgrims from all over Tibet and from cities and towns in India.

The south is known as the granary of Tibet and it is in the fertile valleys that the rice and barley are grown which form the Tibetans' staple food. But even here, where the great ranges run down to the plains of India, the precipitous mountain trails are difficult and dangerous, winding across sheer slopes thousands of feet above raging rivers. More heavily populated than either the north or west, the distances between the villages are usually so great that the rare traveller is often stranded before he can reach human habitation and he dies in the merciless cold.

All the charm of Tibet is concentrated in the east. The great ranges and snow-bound passes still abound—there are thirteen passes over fifteen thousand feet between the comparatively short distance of Batang and Kangting (Tachienlu) alone—but the eye-defeating plateaux are often knee-deep in grass or carpeted with an exotic variety of flowers. Great coniferous forests plunge from the snow line at nineteen thousand feet to valley floors lapping the rivers. To the north-east in Amdo Province there are more plateaux than mountains and rivers but in the south-east, in Kham, or 'Medo Yul' (the Land of Flowers), as it is sometimes called, the eternally snow-crowned Minya Konka, and the other lesser-known but equally beautiful ranges, jealously enclose indescribably beautiful valleys with white-washed villages startling against the dark green forests, tens of thousands of black goat-hair tents with hundreds of thousands of quietly grazing yaks, cattle, goats and sheep.

Everything in Tibet seems unreal. The completely barren plateaux stretching into shimmering infinity; the towering mind-staggering virgin snow-crowned ranges etched sharply against an impossibly blue sky; the great snow-filled plateaux smooth in an unbroken tablecloth of white, then rising in waves of milk to join the peaks; trees, trees, trees, coniferous and deciduous, separated only by rivers or snow or mountain until the mind boggles at the magnitude of their total. Yet everything is separate and distinct, every leaf and flower, every blade of grass and snow crystal, every stone, flashing spray of water and mountain outline is caught and held in a crystallized eternal moment in the rarefied high altitudes.

Almost with the same abruptness with which the mountains fall into the plains on all sides of the country Tibetans differ from their neighbours. The people belong to what is loosely termed the Tartar branch of the human race, and are related in physical type to the peoples of the steppes and deserts to the north, but there, apart from religion, all similarity ceases.

Certainly they borrowed the Buddhism of India and China, but they gave it a character of its own. Their spoken language was adapted to the Indian-acquired Sanskrit, but the speech was derived from Burmese-Polynesian roots. Chinese dress, eating and writing habits were copied from China in the aristocratic circles but the majority of the people retained their own simple food of tsamba (barley flour) and dried meat, their wool-lined goatskin gown, and the living habits of centuries. The Indians were small and brown, the Chinese small and yellow but the Tibetans were tall, magnificently built, fearless and warlike.

The rugged country, the spare, open-air life was responsible for producing such a physically superb people. The rain clouds which sweep across India unload themselves in torrential monsoons on the gigantic ranges of the Himalayas and never reach Tibet. Two hundred inches of rain a year, or more, fall on the Indian side of the eastern Himalayas but only about seven inches fall in Tibet. The greater part of Tibet is icebound seven or eight months of the year, great blizzards sweep over some parts of it from time to time, strong winds rise in the later afternoon and are especially violent in spring and winter, but throughout the year sunshine is the rule except during July and August. Even the inhabited areas can be cultivated for a few months only.

In Central Tibet, where the estates of the nobles and land-owners are, the political system was feudal, but in the east it was still tribal. Tribes and families warred with each other, and raided the caravans passing from China to India. The people are mostly nomads and, to a lesser degree, farmers. Many were small trades-men. An ordinary caravan journey from India to China took six months, and the thousands of muleteers occupied in this way were given one mule in every ten for their own trading purposes. After three years they were taken off by their chieftain and allowed to farm, soldier, or return to their tents.

Until quite recently the Chinese Communists claimed that there were only 1·2 million inhabitants in Tibet, although Sir Charles Bell and others reckoned that there were between three and five million. No census has ever been taken, but Sir Charles Bell, who was a meticulous scholar, took the number of monks, which was estimated at about a hundred thousand, and computing that there was one monk to every three, or perhaps five, lay male inhabitants, arrived at his figure of three to five million.

Only a few months ago I had cause to doubt this figure. While questioning leading Tibetans about the large number of Tibetans being killed in the fighting in Tibet, I casually mentioned Sir Charles Bell's estimated population. The Tibetans immediately rejected this figure, and claimed that there were between ten and twenty million people in Tibet. One of the Tibetans was a leading scholar and I asked him how he arrived at this figure. He claimed that the ratio of monks to lay was nearer one in a hundred or even two hundred. When I doubted this he took a snap count from several of the Tibetans present, who were of the leading aristo-cratic families and large landowners and, true enough, it worked

35

out at between one to one hundred or one hundred and fifty. The vast country, with its inaccessible valleys, can hide innumerable people impossible to estimate, and all those who have produced figures have done so in Lhasa, the capital, where monks are as out of proportion to the lay population as in the Vatican City, if not more so, while two-thirds of Tibet's population is in the east where few have ever travelled.

Before Buddhism was introduced Tibet was a nation of powerful chiefs, warring with each other, and occasionally banding together to sweep down on the foot-hills to the west, south and east of Tibet. After Buddhism was introduced, between the seventh and eleventh centuries, its already decadent form was further impermeated by the nature worship of early Tibetan practices, known as Bön, allied to the shamanism of Central Asia. From being one of the chief military powers of Asia, the nation degenerated into a superstitious, fear-ridden, magic-loving, lama-dominated people. The lamas multiplied rapidly and soon usurped authority in matters of state, finally gaining full control, overthrowing the king in favour of a king from amongst themselves.

Buddhism, or Lamaism as it is more correctly called, has now become almost completely mechanical. Prayers are written on strips of paper and enclosed in little wheels that are turned by hand. Large cylinders outside monasteries are turned by hand or even driven by water power, each containing many thousands of prayers or sacred writings. Long and small prayer flags flutter in the breeze from outside every house and monastery and from every cairn on top of a pass. The rosary of a hundred and eight beads is used by almost every man, woman and child, priesthood and laity.

In every nomad encampment, village, town and city there are monasteries or chapels, and in almost every hut and house there is a family altar where little bowls filled with butter burn as offerings for the dead and living.

The ordinary monastery is usually small, dark, dirty and evil-smelling, with grime-covered religious murals on the smoke-darkened walls. In the gloom large brass images of Buddha and his disciples are barely discernible in the flickering light thrown

upwards from the scores of butter lamps. Dirty *katas*, or ceremonial scarves, are draped from the images' necks, where some
supplicant has hung them perhaps years before.

The larger monasteries are magnificent places. Built usually on
some prominent outcrop, they dominate the town or valley with
their startling white-washed frontage, colourful rafters and gleaming golden roofs and spires. Inside the main hall is a gigantic
golden Buddha, with his disciples on either side, and the halls are
covered with magnificent murals or brocade-bordered *tankas*, or
religious scrolls. The sound of brazen gongs, deep trumpets,
intoning voices and the measured beat of drums is ever present.

In the monasteries there are usually three to five services daily,
lasting four or five hours altogether, for it is there rather than in
the home that religious observance takes place. The monks learn
their prayers and sacred writings by rote and commit them to
memory, and, depending on their repertoire, they will be called in
to pray on the occasion of births, marriages, travel, trade and
deaths. Very few of the lama monks ever really learn to understand
what they read and the percentage of literacy among them is a
great deal lower than is generally thought from watching them
scan their books.

While the Tibetans, like all Buddhists, are supposed to respect
the sanctity of life, and not to kill, they are great meat-eaters and
fighters. They get round the precepts by a cunningly worked-out
system of indulgences for those who have to butcher. In the
tribes of East Tibet, where I have seen fierce warriors take a louse
from their hair and put it carefully out of harm's way, I have
watched these same men sharpen their swords and oil their guns
with loving care in preparation for a battle.

On this great country no other country has made any significant
impact. But where for a thousand years Tibet's relations with the
north, west and south have been, by and large, amicable, to the
east she has never been reconciled. Over the centuries, as the ambitious, tireless Chinese have continued to absorb Tibet within
their sphere of influence, there has grown up in Tibet a steady,
stubborn flame of antagonism towards them. The Mongols came
and went away, and so did the Nepalese and the British, but al-

ways the Chinese came to conquer, take control, alter customs and seek to absorb the country into China. Time after time the Tibetans would drive out the alien Chinese only to find fifty years later that they were back with their endless intrigues, to subjugate Tibet and attach it indissolubly to China.

In Central and West Tibet the feeling against China was not so strong, for there the Tibetans hardly ever saw the Chinese except in Lhasa, but in the east where the fierce independent tribesmen roamed on the borders of China there was constant strife. To the cultured, sophisticated Chinese these warring tribesmen were barbarians, and they were accordingly treated with contempt when they came into trading contact with the Chinese in the border towns. The Kham and Amdo Tibetans responded by attacking any Chinese who ventured beyond the racial boundary of Greater Tibet, from Lanchow through Tachienlu to Atuntze, either for trade or on official journeys to Lhasa, so that the Chinese could travel only under escort from garrison to garrison along the Tachienlu-Batang-Chamdo-Lhasa trade route.

It was into this country that General 'Butcher' Chao Erh-feng marched in 1904–10 to subjugate it once and for all and bring it under the direct control of China. With their Dalai Lama gone, their monasteries burned, their chiefs deposed and Chinese magistrates in their place, it looked as if the Chinese were about to accomplish their centuries-old ambition to annexe Tibet.

In 1910 Chao proposed that Gyamda Dzong, beyond the Salween-Brahmaputra divide, and within a few days' march of Lhasa, should be the new boundary between China and Tibet. Peking at first refused its consent to the proposal but agreed about a year later.

When Chao finally left in August 1911, the work begun in 1905 was outwardly completed, and there was not a Tibetan ruler left in East Tibet. From Tachienlu up to the Mekong the country was actually being administered by Chinese district magistrates, while north of the Mekong and Salween several districts had also been planned but not actually established. When Chao was killed in the revolution in China the same year, his assistant took over and his first act was a proposal that East Tibet should be converted into a new Chinese Province, to be called (H)Sikang, or Western Kham. The revolution against the Manchu dynasty broke out in Szechuan while this proposal was in Chengtu on its way to Peking. Here are some extracts from this remarkable transaction.

'The frontier territory lies between Szechuan in the east and Tibet in the west, and bounded by the Kokonor Territory in the north and Yunnan Province in the south. It was formerly divided up into more than twenty native states and tribes, the inhabitants of which, while paying tribute to the Emperor, *were not actually Chinese subjects* (italics mine). . . . The time has now come when the whole region should be converted into a regular province, which should be named Hsikang. . . . By converting the frontier regions of Kham into a Chinese province we shall secure ourselves against territorial aggression. . . .'

The whole edifice of Chinese control in this vast, simmeringly antagonistic country, however, was only a hastily constructed framework imposed on an unwilling people taken by surprise, and the greater part of it collapsed completely when put to the test at the time of the revolution in China in 1911.

The revolution in China was not immediately followed by uprisings in East Tibet, but gradually, as the Tibetan tribesmen began to realize the significance of the relaxing of Chinese control, they began a series of revolts against the Chinese in Chatreng, Gonjo, Draya, Markham and Chamdo.

By the summer of 1912 the Chinese had lost control of most of the districts in East Tibet. The news filtered through to Lhasa. The Chinese soldiers threw off restraint and began looting and killing, to which the Tibetans retaliated and drove the Chinese out of Central Tibet. By the end of 1912 Chinese authority had ceased to exist in Tibet. The Dalai Lama returned from his exile in India and the country reverted once more to its normal autonomous state.

CHAPTER 4

Tibetan Government

As the campaign against the Chinese mounted in intensity the Tibetans looked like recovering all the territory they had ever inhabited and claimed in the East up to Tachienlu. There was, too, a very real danger that they might sweep beyond. The Chinese finally appealed to Britain to mediate, and the British Government told the Dalai Lama, through Sir Charles Bell, that Tibet should stop fighting. The Dalai Lama was very angry. He felt much as the nations of the West feel about Mr. Nehru, Indian Prime Minister, when he applies the principle of neutrality more to the Western bloc than to the Communist. For while China was killing Tibetans, burning monasteries, killing officials and altering administration Britain did not interfere, yet as soon as the Tibetans started defending their country, reclaiming their territory, and defeating the Chinese in doing so, the British stepped in at the request of the Chinese to stop them.

In 1912 the Dalai Lama returned to Tibet. The doctrine of *Karma* had been fulfilled in the retribution which had fallen upon the Manchu Emperor of China for the traitorous way in which he treated his spiritual preceptor, the Dalai Lama, and the innocent people of Tibet. The Dalai Lama's own lesser spiritual discipline in the two years of exile known to the Tibetans as 'Interruption' to be made good by religious exercises, was at an end. Of this he wrote in his political testament: 'Religious services were held on behalf of the Faith and the secular side of state affairs. These ensured the full ripening of the evil deeds of the Chinese, and in consequence internal commotion broke out in China, and the time was changed.' When the President of the new Chinese Republic telegraphed to him apologizing for the excesses of the Chinese troops and restoring the Dalai Lama to his former rank, the Dalai Lama replied that he was not asking the Chinese Government for any rank and that he intended to exercise both secular and ecclesiastical rule in Tibet.

To describe the constitution of the Government in Tibet in a few words is not easy, for over the centuries it emerged, was altered, was abolished and reconstituted until it was difficult to fit into any pattern. Briefly, the Supreme Government consists of the Dalai Lama at the top, then the Chief Minister, and then the Cabinet of one priest and three laymen. Next comes the Ecclesiastical Court which deals with matters concerning the large body of monks in the country, and below this the National Assembly or Parliament.

The Cabinet is known as the 'Kashag', and each Cabinet member is known as a 'Shape'. The Kashag has a general controlling power over the internal administration of the country, whether in political, revenue or judicial matters. Both the Cabinet and the Ecclesiastical Court send their more important reports to the Dalai Lama through the Chief Minister.

The National Assembly, or 'Tsong-du', the Tibetan equivalent of Parliament, is composed of all secular and ecclesiastical officials below the members of the Kashag, or such of them as happen to be stationed in Lhasa. The total number of officials in Tibet is usually around three hundred and fifty, half of them lay and half ecclesiastical.

The place of assembly is a large hall in a temple near the Kashag offices. Part of the room is higher than the rest and on the raised portion sit those who hold the superior position of Kung, Dzasa, and Techi, as well as the Grand Secretaries and Finance Secretaries. The Grand Secretaries are the four heads of the Ecclesiastical Court and the Finance Secretaries are the three heads from among the lay members. The Grand Secretaries and the Finance Secretaries do most of the talking, the priests usually more than the laymen, in the form of general discussion rather than in speeches on prepared subjects. Decisions are not put to the vote, but from the way that the discussion goes the minority opinion will gradually drop out and the conclusion be arrived at by those who hold the floor. After the Assembly has come to a decision it is reported verbally to the Cabinet, who pass it on with their opinion to the Minister, and he in turn communicates it to the Dalai Lama. Usually no written record is kept of the proceedings.

Up to the twentieth century the Assembly exercised great power in Tibet. During the interregnum between Dalai Lamas when a Regent was in power the Assembly was strong enough to prevent the Regent from dominating the country. In the twentieth century the Thirteenth Dalai Lama, like his famous predecessor, the Great Fifth, took over almost complete control of the secular and ecclesiastical administration and cleverly manipulated the Assembly to accept his personal views.

However, with all its ceremonial and outwardly impressive procedure, the Lhasa or Central Government exercised power only in the limited region of Central Tibet. To the north Ladakh, while theoretically Tibetan, felt very little official impact from Lhasa, although its priests and traders plied constantly between the two provinces. In the east there was practically no influence exercised amongst the tribesmen of Kham and Amdo, except when some strong Lhasa Government official was in Chamdo who would use his authority to collect taxes or bribes.

The chief difficulty in governing Tibet from the centre was due to the long distances that had to be travelled over the high passes and deep gorges. A normal journey from Lhasa to the outlying provinces usually took about three months. Communications were difficult and the cost of trying to enforce decisions prohibitive.

The Dalai Lama maintained his own intelligence service so that he knew most of what went on throughout the country and was not dependent on the information given to him by his leading government officials. In addition he would give private audiences to selected individuals. Officials were, accordingly, never quite sure how much he knew on any subject at any time, and they pursued a cautious policy. Thus he was not just an isolated impotent religious head of state. In fact, a Tibetan proverb concerning the Dalai Lama reads: 'If he tells you to strike a rock, strike! If he tells you to go to hell, go!'

Tibetan Government

The machinery of government, primitive and feudal as it was, became further complicated by the fact that positions were usually inherited or bought—a Shape's position cost about seven lakhs of rupees, or £50,000. Many government posts were held on contract, and could be rented out to someone else for a period, so that a posting to an unpopular frontier district could often be avoided by sending some other official or relative while the person concerned remained in Lhasa or on his estate.

The Tibetan noble or official from Lhasa is a charming person to meet, smiling, courteous, hospitable and friendly, particularly if one has taken the trouble to learn Tibetan. But very few of them are keen to put in any hard work for the Government until there is some crisis. They will attend parties, play mahjong, visit each other and chat for hours, go on picnics, attend ceremonies, watch horse races or sports, but they will do little or nothing towards applying themselves to study or work.

In the past twenty years many of them have sent their sons and daughters to be educated in India. These now form the younger generation of officials who speak and read fluent English. Many newspapers and magazines are now received in Lhasa to keep them informed of what is going on in the outside world; but outside of Lhasa, until the Chinese Communist invasion in 1950, this increase in education and knowledge made little impact on the country.

Until recently it was considered *infra dig.* for a Tibetan noble or official to learn to read or write. Scribes recruited from the monasteries were kept for this purpose, for only in the monasteries was there any semblance of education, and this was given only to the monks in training. Quite apart from the spiritual benefits to be derived from entering the priesthood, the secular rewards were also considerable. An ambitious monk could work himself up through the monastic system to a position of power and influence, not only over the district but over the country as well. The abbots of the three large monasteries in Lhasa—Sera, Drepung and Ganden, totalling over twenty thousand monks—had considerable influence on the Assembly, the Kashag and even on the Dalai Lama.

Tibetan Government

The monasteries in the main are exempt from taxation, and they receive vast revenues from estates which they own and from offerings by their religious followers. Landowners too are often exempt from taxation, for little or no reason, but they often make payments in kind to the Government (in butter or grain), and they take only a nominal salary for their Government work. Ordinary people, farmers and labourers, throughout the country must supply transport and porterage free of charge.

In addition to the treasury of grain and butter there are the Dalai Lama's own private treasury from Government, estates and gifts, the 'reserve treasury' of gold, corals, diamonds and silver to meet the possible demands of war, famine or other calamities, and a fourth treasury for the Army. There is no income-tax in Tibet, no excise levies and practically no customs duties.

Most of the wealth of Tibet came originally from the provinces of Kham and Amdo in East Tibet, as that is the most populous and fertile part of the country. The Chinese move into this area, therefore, the forcible taking over, under Chao Erh-feng, of its administration, became a matter of grave financial importance to the Lhasa Government.

Prior to this annexation by the Chinese and the redirecting of the East Tibet taxation revenue to Peking, the Kham and Amdo Tibetans had paid taxes through their rulers, chiefs and monasteries to the Lhasa Government, reluctantly but recognizing the necessity. So long as direct interference in their lives by the Lhasa Government was kept at a minimum they felt little need to do more than grumble at having to pay taxes. In any case, they were so busy fighting amongst themselves, banding together only to pull down some chieftain who looked like becoming too powerful, that they gave little thought to the possibility that they were sufficiently powerful to oppose and even overthrow the weak Government in Lhasa.

The official Tibetan Army was a Gilbertian affair, recruited from the estates of the great landowners. Each landed proprietor had annually to supply soldiers for the army in accordance with the amount and fertility of his land, plus two complete outfits of clothing, boots, etc., for the soldiers. The Government paid the soldiers only in grain and a little cash. Until World War II there were no more than about ten thousand regular soldiers in the Tibetan Army, mostly supplied with World War I rifles, a few cannon and machine-guns. But during the war the army was reorganized and increased to fifteen thousand in fifteen regiments. Districts had to supply their contingents with provisions and supplementary pay, and the Government introduced regular organization and established fixed rates of pay for officers and men.

Most of the army was kept in Lhasa and in the towns in West Tibet. Only a few hundred were sent to Chamdo and other 'dzongs' or garrisons in the east. When, in 1912, the revolution in China had settled down, the Chinese sent a force of some five thousand Chinese to try to retrieve the position in East Tibet. The Chinese General recaptured Tachienlu, Batang and Chamdo, and by 1914 Chinese control had been to a great extent established in the frontier regions.

The Lhasa Government, having regained their autonomy, were determined to retain it, and the Commander-in-Chief of the Tibetan Army was sent with troops into Kham to stop the Chinese advance. From then on the situation on the frontier changed and what had been confused border warfare between Lhasa Government soldiers, Kham tribesmen and monks, and Chinese troops developed into a war between China and Tibet over the question of the Sino-Tibetan frontier.

A tripartite conference was convoked at Simla in India to try to settle the dispute. The Tibetan delegate not only demanded independence, an indemnity, and the right to denounce the Anglo-Chinese Convention of 1906 and to amend the Trade Regulations of 1893 and 1908, but he insisted on the return to Tibet of all the land as far as Tachienlu and the extension of Tibetan territory to include Kokonor.

China suggested that land north of the Dangla Range should belong to Chinghai Province with the original boundary maintained; Batang, Litang and Atuntze should be regarded as a part of China proper under direct Chinese rule; while the land east of the Salween river including Derge, Nyarong, and the territory of the Thirty-nine Tribes should form a special district called Kham.

Britain compromised by suggesting that the land north-east of the Dzachuka Range (or Kokonor), Chinchuan (in Szechuan), Tachienlu and Atuntze (in Yunnan) would be put under Chinese rule, while Nyarong and Derge should be turned over to Inner Tibet. No Chinese troops were to be stationed within three hundred miles of Lhasa, and they had to be withdrawn beyond the Amne Machin mountain range in north-east Tibet. China's suzerainty over the whole of Tibet was to be recognized together with the autonomy of Outer Tibet. Both Britain and China were to respect the territorial integrity of the country and to abstain from interference in the administration of Outer Tibet, which was to remain in the hands of the Tibetan Government at Lhasa. China was forbidden to send troops or civilian officials into that region except for a Resident at Lhasa with an escort of not more than three hundred men. She was not to colonize Tibet. Tibet would not be represented in the Chinese Parliament or any other similar body. China had to pledge that she would not convert Tibet into a province.

The Draft Convention was initialled in April 1914 by the three delegates preparatory to signature. Two days after the Draft of the Convention had been initialled the Chinese Government telegraphed repudiating it, but Tibet and Britain recognized it as binding on themselves. The concluding words of the Treaty are:

'This being the Independent Treaty entered into by the Government of Great Britain in India and the Government of Tibet by mutual agreement.

'The Government of Great Britain in India and the Government of Tibet by mutual consent consider as ratified and come into force the preceeding Treaty of this same day.

'The Government of China refusing to affix her official seal thereto, and in default of which, all rights and privileges claimed by the Government of China in and with regard to Tibet, are hereby declared revoked.'

The Dalai Lama objected to the proposal for the division of Tibet into two, Inner and Outer, but accepted it reluctantly when Bell pointed out that so long as the name Tibet was retained, when the Tibetan Army grew strong enough to insist on Tibet's rights they could regain possession of this part of the country. The Indian Government under Prime Minister Nehru, as revealed by Chinese Ambassador Lo Chia-lun, in 1950 declared to the Chinese Government that it recognized only the validity of the Simla Convention of 1914.

In East Tibet, though, the matter of Chinese relations could not be settled by discussions in India, or even in Lhasa, the fierce and independent Kham Tibetans having nothing to do with the political expediences which made them Chinese subjects. In 1915 the Khambas again rose in revolt and, capturing Tachienlu, they emerged on Szechuan Province.

The central government at Peking and the provincial government of Szechuan were too preoccupied with internal civil wars in China to pay any attention to the Tibetan border, and the Chinese soldiers garrisoned there were left to their own devices. For some obscure reason the Chinese General decided to march on Lhasa. After a long siege lasting several months in Chamdo, he was defeated and forced to capitulate.

By the middle of 1918 the Tibetans had recovered all of East Tibet from the Chinese garrisons, and were ready to reclaim all their former territory up to and including Tachienlu. At this juncture, however, the Chinese invoked the mediation of the British Consular Agent stationed in West China, and on his intervention the Tibetans were persuaded to stop fighting.

Peace negotiations followed and arrangements were finally concluded providing for the cessation of hostilities and the mutual withdrawal of the troops of both sides. A provisional boundary coinciding to a considerable extent with the old seventeenth-century line of the Manchus was drawn up, and the frontier region settled down once again.

However, the Lhasa Government, while withdrawing troops from the area and leaving the tribesmen under their native rulers and chiefs, brought to a head the growing irritation of the tribesmen of East Tibet with the Lhasa officials. Having been the means of clearing the country of the Chinese, the Khambas felt that they were due for some recognition or recompense, instead of which the Lhasa Government foolishly imposed on the people of East Tibet a retrospective demand for payment of all taxes due throughout the period of Chinese occupation.

Had government machinery for extracting this been other than through the monasteries there might then have been a revolt against the Government in Lhasa. As it was, the tribesmen had to pay in their usual way to the monasteries, or the headmen to other leading chiefs, so that open conflict was avoided; but the normal bitter feeling against the distant Lhasa officials increased to near-hatred, and the leaders in Kham and Amdo swore that such an imposition would never be tolerated again.

3. & 4. Two types of monastery in Tibet
Above: the active type serving the community
and seat of political intrigue
Below: the isolated type for the spiritually contemplative

5. Kalimpong, in foreground, with Dr. Graham's Homes to the right and 27,000 foot Kanchenjunga behind

CHAPTER 5

East Tibet's Anti-Lhasa Plans

Kham and Amdo tribesmen stand in much the same relation to each other as did the Scots and Irish of two centuries ago. In Kham there were thirty-nine major tribes and in Amdo twenty-five, and they were usually occupied fighting each other or raiding each other's property and territory. The only time they stopped their inter-tribal fighting was to unite against the invading Chinese or against the Lhasa Government officials and soldiers.

Normally cheerful and friendly, frank and hospitable, they would fight at the slightest challenge for the sheer love of battle. They were completely fearless, courting death in the most reckless manner, this arising partly from their natural courage and partly from their belief in their religious charms and observances. They used rifles and revolvers in their battles but preferred in-fighting with swords, riding with reckless skill on fast mountain ponies in attack on their enemies, disconcerting them with the shock of attack and then hacking their way through against incredible odds. They were also excellent marksmen, who were brought up on rifle practice from early adolescence, and their opening salvoes before riding out caused widespread death and panic. Their rulers and chieftains were not of the weak inbred hereditary type so common in Lhasa, but men who had emerged from the rank and file by virtue of their courage, strength and prowess. Only when these men looked like becoming too ambitious, or too strong, did the other tribes unite to defeat them in battle.

This jealously guarded independence permitted the astute Chinese to exert their divide-and-rule policy so often in East Tibet. Provided there were no widespread use of force, the

D   49

Tibetans of Kham and Amdo usually ignored the existence of Chinese garrisons and magistrates' offices in a few towns, where these had no influence over the Tibetans' daily lives.

They considered themselves Tibetans, of the same family as their fellow-countrymen in Central Tibet, but of a superior breed. They were not obsequious to their own officials, unlike the oppressed serfs in Central Tibet; they were warriors, free men who of their own choice had submitted themselves to follow their respective chiefs. Most of them grew up, and many spent their whole lives, without ever seeing a single Chinese or Lhasa official.

It is an interesting historical speculation that they might have continued indefinitely in their simple tribal living, growing into a separate minority racial unit of their own in such a vast territory, had it not been for the identifying and unifying factor of their religion. Forming two-thirds of Greater Tibet's population, and many of the males entering the priesthood, a steady stream of them passed through the monasteries, either on pilgrimage or for further studies, to Lhasa. This steady passing to and fro not only cemented them into religious harmony but into a racial entity as well, and the influence that so many of them wielded as leaders in the affairs of the three large monasteries in Lhasa over secular and religious affairs gave them, their relatives and fellow-countrymen in Kham and Amdo, a taste of possibly even greater power were they, instead of the hereditary Lhasa officials, in control of the whole country.

Between 1920 and 1930 the Lhasa Government grew cool towards the British Government and turned once again to China. This was a surprising and inexplicable development for it was during the period of the Dalai Lama's close friendship with Sir Charles Bell and while China was weak and divided and in no position to threaten Tibet. However, the honeymoon period was finally brought to an end and once more it was in Kham that the trouble began.

The incident started over a dispute in the Kanze district of Kham, near Tachienlu. A quarrel developed between the abbot of a monastery and the new headman of a village. The abbot called in the monks and occupied the village. The Chinese garrison intervened and clashed with the monks. Reinforcements were sent from Lhasa and China and a major conflict flared up again.

The situation was further confused by the weak control which the Central Government of China had over the generals in the Western Province who acted as war-lords and very often disregarded orders from the Central Government in Nanking.

The Commander-in-Chief of the Sikang garrison forces was a General Liu Wen-huie, one of the worst types of the notorious war-lords and hated by the Tibetans. Consequently, when he marched in with his troops to settle the dispute the whole region, helped by four thousand troops from Lhasa, rose up in revolt once again.

The Chinese Nationalist Government was in no position to enforce its will on Tibet, for in addition to the difficulties of warfare in such mountainous terrain the Chinese garrison troops had degenerated into little better than town toughs and bandits. Even Liu Wen-huie's troops, originally from Szechuan, although better equipped and better fed, were not much better disciplined.

It was easy, therefore, for the popular Kham Tibetan leader, Kesang Tsering, the Chinese-recognized Commissioner for Kuomintang Affairs for Sikang, with the support of local Tibetans, to disarm the local garrison in Batang in 1932 and establish an autonomous régime which covered most of Kham. In the same year the garrison in Tachienlu mutinied, and the General, Ma Su, was put to death.

On December 17, 1933, the Dalai Lama died. He had been a controversial figure during his lifetime, having taken so much secular authority into his own hands, but he had put down bribery and corruption, imposed law and order, strengthened his own contact with his people, introduced new merciful standards into the administration of justice and lessened priestly domination in secular affairs. To prevent Chinese invasions he had built up an army in the face of opposition by priests who feared for their power if the military grew too strong, and he had abolished Chinese domination, making Tibet a completely independent nation.

What he did not do was leave prophetic instructions regarding his incarnation in a fourteenth Dalai Lama. Before his death rumours had been circulating widely that the line of reincarnation of the Dalai Lama was to cease with the thirteenth, after which would come a drastic change of Government. As the Thirteenth Dalai Lama had not provided the usual information about the exact location of his next appearance on earth, doubts were expressed even in monastic circles as to whether there would ever be another Dalai Lama.

To make matters worse, the younger Tibetans who were anxious for reform wanted to continue the Dalai Lama's policy of extending military powers and diminishing priestly control. All this was further complicated by the usual noble families contesting for influence during the interregnum.

The chief target of ambition was the post of Regent, the occupant of which would be in control of political and religious affairs until the majority of the new Dalai Lama. Through the co-operation of the monks, and the public demand that the regency should go to a priest and not to a layman, it was finally decided that Reting Hutukhtu, the abbot of Reting monastery, two days' march from Lhasa, should be Regent. He was appointed in January, 1934.

They were dangerous times, for in Lhasa there were shifts of power as the late Dalai Lama's nephew struggled with Kunpel-La, the Dalai Lama's favourite, for control, and the powerful 'Kingmaker', Tsarong, the Commander-in-Chief, tried to seize the reins of government but failed to get the necessary backing from Sera and other monasteries.

East Tibet also had felt the repercussions and the possibilities in the new situation. Geshi Sherab Gyaltso, a leading Amdo monk, had to flee from Lhasa for his part in the intrigue there, and on retiring to his home in Amdo joined forces with another Amdo Tibetan chieftain, Lobsang Tsewong, also commonly known as Abu Abolok and by his Chinese cognomen of Hou Wan Seiling, to organize revolt against the centre.

Meanwhile in Kham, to the south of Amdo, an ambitious young chieftain, Pangdatshang Topgyay, who was military Governor of Markham, and his older brother, Pangdatshang Rapga, decided that the time had come for the Khambas to strike. They hastily got together a force of a few thousand Khambas and marched on Chamdo, the chief city of East Tibet, en route to Lhasa. Here their ambitions were thwarted, for they were betrayed by the monks of Chamdo Monastery who already had plans of their own.

While the Pangdatshang brothers were falling back before the Tibetan Army, supplemented by other chieftains united with the Batang Tibetan officials against the Pangdatshangs, the Chinese became disturbed at such a large force of armed Tibetans on the Chinese frontiers and despatched an army. The Pangdatshang brothers were defeated by the combined forces of Central Tibetans and Chinese, but by a clever ruse both brothers escaped to India via Hong Kong.

The possibility of civil war in Tibet did not finish with this, however, and a new danger of civil war arose when the Chinese decided that it would be a good time for the Panchen Lama, who had fled to China a few years earlier, to return to Tibet. In the eyes of the Lhasa authorities this constituted an immediate danger threatening their very existence.

In February, 1934, the Panchen Lama had been sworn in as a member of the National Government of China. In other words, he was admitted to the Supreme Council, the highest Chinese honour he could possibly receive. On February 8, 1935, he had been appointed 'Special Cultural Commissioner for the Western Regions', with his headquarters in Sining, in the Chinese province of Chinghai. The Chinese General had persuaded the Regent Reting to give his reluctant consent to the Panchen Lama's return, and in March 1937 he arrived in Jyekundo, in Amdo, on his way to Shigatse, via Nagchuka, so that he would not go near Lhasa.

When the news reached Lhasa, however, the Government decided that they would oppose his return with armed resistance. While the situation was still tense, and negotiations were proceeding in Lhasa, Nanking, Delhi and London, the Panchen Lama fell ill. He died in Jyekundo in December 1937.

The death of the Panchen Lama removed a major source of friction and possible revolt in Tibet. But the temporary *rapprochement* was obviated by the later Chinese activities in relation to the discovery and removal of the new Dalai Lama.

The discovery of a new Dalai Lama is one of the most remarkable processes in this remarkable country. The Dalai Lama is celibate and when he dies he has no heir and no official successor. But it is believed that within a year or two after his death he chooses to return to earth to help humanity and he enters some womb to be reincarnated. It is not true, as is often believed in the West, that the birth is simultaneous with the death.

Sometimes before his death the Dalai Lama in a prophetic utterance will give some indication of where his rebirth might be expected. If this is not forthcoming, and there is confusion following on his death, the State Oracle, the Tibetan equivalent of the ancient Delphic Oracle, will be called in and he will indicate while under spirit possession the district where the new Dalai Lama may be found.

As the Thirteenth Dalai Lama had given no prophetic indication of where he would reincarnate himself, the discovery was left to other processes. Apart from the State Oracle, another method is the use of mystical lakes to divine the mind of the gods or, as it was described to Sir Charles Bell: 'The water of the lake is blue. You watch it from the hillside. A wind arises, and turns the blue water into white. A hole then forms in this white water; the hole is blue-black. Clouds form above this hole, and below the clouds you see images showing future events.'

It was in such a lake that the birthplace of the Fourteenth Dalai Lama was foretold. In an official letter the Regent of Tibet, Reting Hutukhtu, gave the following account of how the new Dalai Lama was discovered:

'When he was born, an image of the house where his parents dwelt appeared in the Holy Lake of Ch'u-ko-chi, and this was later again seen and confirmed by an investigating party headed by myself. Furthermore, various divine omens foretold that he was to be born in the eastern part of Tibet. Yet three parties were sent out in three different directions to make sure that a true reincarnation would be located. The party sent to the east, headed by Chi-ts'ang (Kyi-tsang) Hutukhtu, at first had found fourteen male children who bore extraordinary omens and rare appearances. Among these was this boy by the name of La-mu-tan-chu, born on the sixth day of the sixth month of the I-hai year (1935), into the family bearing the name of Ch'i, in the vicinity of Kumbum monastery, in Kokonor. At the time of his birth all the people in the same village saw a felicitous rainbow pointing towards his house. Afterwards, when the investigating party arrived at his house, although both the father and the mother had no know-ledge of the Tibetan language,* the little boy was very happy to see the party and uttered words in the Tibetan dialect. Then he was tested by four articles which had been in daily use by the Dalai Lama, each of the four articles having a replica. The boy picked up the genuine one in each case. Therefore, all the people ecclesiastical and secular, rich and poor, old and young, sincerely believed that he was the true incarnation of the Thirteenth Dalai Lama.'

He was installed as the Fourteenth Dalai Lama on the fourteenth day of the first month by the Tibetan calendar (February 21, 1940). He was only four-and-a-half years old when he was installed, but he conducted himself with quiet dignity throughout the cere-monies lasting for several days.

Tibet having proclaimed her independence of China about thirty years earlier, no confirmation of the appointment was sought from China, but the National Government kept a stake in the affair by sending four hundred thousand dollars in Chinese currency to cover expenses for the installation ceremony. Pre-sumably this was to counter some of the ill-feeling created in Tibet when the Chinese Government of Chinghai Province first de-manded one hundred thousand Chinese dollars (£7,500) and later another three hundred and thirty thousand Chinese dollars (£25,000). This official blackmail was paid by the Tibetans but the delay of a year while the negotiations went on generated more bitter feeling against the Chinese throughout the country.

In 1947 there was an attempted *coup d'état* to overthrow the

* This is the superior Lhasa attitude to all dialects spoken outside Central Tibet, and does not mean that the family knew no Tibetan; on the contrary, the family told me that they spoke Amdo Tibetan from birth as they were Amdo Tibetans. Some Tibetan scholars maintain that the dialects spoken in Kham, Amdo and other areas of Greater Tibet are purer Tibetan than that used by the Lhasa officials of Central Tibet, which has become corrupted by terminology borrowed from India and China and by a restricted inbreeding. Author's Note.

Government in Lhasa. Reting, the Regent, had retired to Reting Monastery for a period of contemplation and left the affairs of state in the hands of one Takta Rimpoche. When Reting had completed his time of meditation and was about to return to take up the reins of government, Tagta Rimpoche sent an army to Reting Monastery to arrest the former Regent on a specious charge that he had attempted to take his, the acting Regent's, life. The monks of Sera, who respected Reting, revolted against this action and there was widespread panic. However, Tagta's plans had been well laid, and Reting was secretly taken to the dungeons of the Potala and killed, along with other members of his family and close friends. The army bombarded Lhasa and Sera with howitzers, and the resistance collapsed. Tagta was intensely hated, but he was also feared.

During this time the Tibetans in Kham and Amdo had also been busy. While the war against the Japanese had been going on in China, and when Chiang-Kai-shek had to make his famous retreat to the west with his Government he had had the idea of bringing in the Kham and Amdo Tibetans as a last line of defence. Accordingly, he promoted to the position of honorary Colonel, responsible for leading the Khambas against the Japanese if called upon to do so, Pangdatshang Topgyay, who had led the earlier revolt against Lhasa and then fled, but who had returned and with his brothers was now one of the leading traders in Central Asia. Abu Abolok (Lobsang Tsewong), the Tibetan leader in Amdo, was made a General, and responsible for the Amdo Tibetans.

Not only did these appointments serve to bring the Kham and Amdo Tibetans into a unity they had never had before—neither Topgyay nor Lobsang Tsewong was suspect as pro-Chinese for they had not been asked to concede anything other than willingness to fight against the Japanese—but, much more important, it gave them access to unlimited supplies of modern weapons, which were easily available to them in their new official capacity as possible fighters with China, or unofficially through the gun-running channels operated by the war-lord generals in the border provinces.

The opportunity was too good to be passed over and the Kham

and Amdo leaders got together and began making plans to over-throw the Central Government in Lhasa. The leaders of the East Tibetan revolutionaries were the two Amdo Tibetans, Lobsang Tsewong and Geshi Sherab Gyaltso, the rebel monk who had fled from Lhasa, and the two Kham Tibetans, the Pangdatshang brothers, Topgyay and Rapga, who had led the revolt against Chamdo a few years before and then later fought a losing battle against the Chinese.

Topgyay had only spent a few months in Kalimpong, on the Indian-Tibetan border, under an assumed name and disguised as a trader, after which he returned to Tibet and China with the help of his eldest brother, Yangpel, head of the Pangdatshang family and trading concern in Lhasa. Rapga had chosen to stay on in Kalimpong. Here he applied himself to studying English and politics, and as his knowledge of these improved, to translating into Tibetan such works as Sun Yat Sen's *San Min Chu-i* or *Three Principles of the People*, and excerpts from Karl Marx and International Law. He wrote political articles for the Tibetan news-paper published in Kalimpong, *The Tibet Mirror Press*, and asso-ciated himself with the Indian Congress Party in its struggle with Britain for independence.

In 1943 he was joined in Kalimpong by another famous Tibetan, Kunpel-La, the former Dalai Lama's favourite, who had been arrested, imprisoned and had escaped through Bhutan to Kalimpong. In Kalimpong Kunpel-La, who at one period had controlled the whole of Tibet under the Thirteenth Dalai Lama, was reduced to working as a manager of a warehouse storing Tibetan wool.

After Kunpel-La's arrival in Kalimpong Chinese Kuomingtang officials, seeing in him a useful discontented element, tried to per-suade him to go to China where they would pay him a salary. However, he was more interested in Rapga's suggestion that they form a Democratic Reform Party to overthrow the old priest-controlled régime in Lhasa and take over power in Tibet. They certainly had contacts with China but had no intention of submitting themselves or Tibet to Chinese control.

As it was Britain's policy at the time to keep Tibet a buffer state, and to preserve the *status quo* of the old conservative régime, they declared Rapga and Kunpel-La 'undesirable elements' with 'terrorist' proclivities and Chinese associations and expelled them from India to China.

In China Rapga became a member of the Commission for Mongolian and Tibetan Affairs and a delegate for Kham to the Chinese National Assembly. Although he held these positions in China Rapga hoped that he might ultimately be successful in his ambition of a representative government for the whole of Tibet, Kham and Amdo included, with friendly links with India and China. When Chiang Kai-shek finally intimated to him his policy of the ultimate absorption of Tibet into China, Rapga voluntarily surrendered his appointments and declared his resignation publicly in the Chinese newspaper *Takung Pao* of February 27, 1948. He then returned to Tachienlu, or Kangting as it had been renamed, in Kham, to join his brother Topgyay.

Here he was able to modify some of the more extreme ambitions of the Kham and Amdo Tibetans by his greater knowledge of Lhasa and international affairs. For instance, Topgyay and several others wanted to march on Lhasa, overthrow the Government and set up a new one from amongst themselves, either in Lhasa or in Chamdo. Rapga urged that it was better to use political pressure first, seeking the Lhasa officials' co-operation in establishing a Greater Tibet with representatives from Kham and Amdo in a new government.

The Khambas were against this moderate policy, depending so much on political manipulation and so little on the military activities they preferred, and were all for compromising on establishing an East Tibetan Government in Kham and Amdo, with the capital and administrative centre in Chamdo. The greatest traders were from Kham, and it was the wealthiest province, also they would command the trade routes into China and would open up a new trade route by-passing Lhasa by going straight from Chamdo through Zayul to Sadiya, in Assam. They felt that this would be sufficient to bring Lhasa to its knees and to agreement.

In the meantime they took every opportunity of buying up guns and ammunition from a rapidly deteriorating China. The monumental corruption which was going on in China provided the West China frontier generals with unlimited possibilities of adding to their private wealth. General Liu Wen-huie, the Governor of Sikang, openly participated in a staggering trade in guns, ammunition and opium, and as the situation worsened it was easier to buy guns and ammunition from any policeman or soldier on the street than it was to buy vegetables. Not only Chinese guns poured into Tibet from China, but all types of modern weapons supplied to China by the allies. I personally saw hundreds of yak caravans carrying guns and ammunition, and huge storehouses in the mountains stocked from floor to ceiling with such equipment. Even monasteries were used to store arms in preparation for the revolt. Armed with these the fierce tribesmen from Kham and Amdo would sweep through the rest of Tibet, including the poorly armed Tibetan Army, with scarcely any opposition.

It must not be thought that because these were tribesmen that what they wanted was a return to tribal barbarism. On the contrary, many of the leaders in the revolt were educated Tibetans who had studied in China and who had learned district administration under Chinese supervision for the past twenty years. Rapga Pangdatshang himself knew more of international politics than the whole of the Lhasa Government put together. Although conditions in Kham and Amdo were much better than in feudal-governed Central Tibet, they wanted to introduce even more sweeping reforms, reducing the power of the monks—which was also less in the east than in the west—and introducing roads, hospitals, schools. Rapga had even drawn up a scheme whereby the priesthood would be divided into eight grades, according to their abilities, and be used through the monasteries as a preliminary education system for Tibet, instead of being just a parasitic growth. Those who did not conform to any of the eight grades were to be forbidden the priesthood and returned to their families and manual labour.

While plans for the revolt were gradually germinating in the vast uncertain area and slow communications of East Tibet, startling news arrived from Lhasa.

In February 1948 a Tibetan trade mission headed by a Lhasa

Finance Secretary, Shakabpa, with colleagues, Surkhang (military) and the eldest Pangdatshang brother, Yangpel (trade), arrived in New Delhi for talks with the Indian Government. The mission then went on to Nanking where the Chinese Nationalist Government tried its utmost to persuade them to take Chinese passports for their intended trip abroad. However, the Tibetans resisted this pressure—as Rapga Pangdatshang had advised—and they visited the United States and Great Britain without the Chinese passports. On the return of the mission to India in 1948 they tried to persuade the Indian Government to support their request for independence. Under pressure from the Chinese the Indian Foreign Minister assured the Chinese Ambassador that there was no such intention on the part of the Indian Government.

On July 8, 1949, the Kashag decided to get rid of all Chinese officials in Lhasa, including those working in the radio station and hospital, and also the teachers in the Chinese primary schools. The Lhasa Government took over the Chinese Government radio station and sealed all its equipment. They forbade any Chinese to send telegraphic messages even through the Indian wireless service. A part of the Chinese personnel left on July 13, and the remainder a week later.

This was shattering news to the Kham and Amdo leaders, for this was a move that they had not anticipated and they felt that behind it there must be British, Indian or American influence. If this were so then it would place their revolt in quite a different perspective, for instead of being an internal affair against a weak reactionary government they might find themselves opposed to the armies of any of the countries mentioned. They were not alone in this belief for General Yen Hsi-shan, the President of the Executive Yuan of the Chinese Nationalist Government, issued a statement in which he implied that the drastic measure was probably not taken by the Lhasa authorities of their own volition.

Communications being what they were in Tibet, and the situation in China having reached the chaotic stage as the Communists overran the country, disrupting all communications there, the leaders of the revolt decided that in the circumstances they could not go ahead with their revolt and would have to wait until events settled down.

CHAPTER 6

Chinese Communists Occupy Tibet

Kangting, until recently Tachienlu, where the Pangdatshangs were living at the time, was a typical border town. With a mixture of races, as might be expected of a terminus of a great Central Asian trade route, it provided a twenty-four hour round of gambling, opium-smoking, sexual satisfaction of all kinds, fighting enough to please even the Khambas, and practically no law enforcement at all.

The Governor of the Province, General Liu Wen-huie, had plans of his own to buy his safety by annexing Szechuan and handing the area over to the advancing Communists. This meant withdrawing what troops he had left from Kham. The remainder, together with the armed police, not being paid, took to raiding and looting the towns and villages of Sikang, east of Kangting. The situation became so bad by mid-1949 that the people of Kangting pleaded with Pangdatshang Topgyay to take over control of the town and province in the interests of law and order. Topgyay was too astute for such an open move, but agreed to be responsible if the Chinese merchants would see that the police were paid. This new danger on his rear worried Liu Wen-huie and he despatched a colonel and detachment of troops to Kangting to head off the expected take-over, and also, if possible, to arrest the Pangdatshang brothers. At the same time Peking announced by radio that they had come to an agreement with the four leaders of the East Tibet revolutionary group and that Kham and Amdo were now the East Tibetan Autonomous Region of the People's Republic.

This was an unexpected move for it meant that not only would it be believed by the world that they had gone over to the Chinese Communists, but also it would be wrongly thought in Lhasa that they were traitors as well as rebels. It was clear that the Chinese were about to approach them with a view to implementing the plan they had already announced as settled.

The Pangdatshang brothers hastily decided to withdraw from points of contact with the Chinese so that they need not be forced to take a hasty and irrevocable decision. Once in the mountains of East Tibet it would take the Chinese several months to reach them with a message or, if the message arrived earlier, they could pretend that it had not and thus they would gain time to sound the reaction of Lhasa and even of the outside powers.

In September 1949, just as General Liu Wen-hiue's troops were arriving, the Pangdatshang brothers left Kangting with an armed escort and proceeded via Litang to Bo, a Pangdatshang stronghold two days south of Batang. On the way tribal chiefs, abbots of monasteries, headmen of villages and nomad encampments and bandit leaders met them to declare their loyalty and the number of men and guns they represented. Over twenty Batang officials came to give a belated apology for their traitorous part in the earlier revolt and to return guns and wealth stolen at the time.

In early January a fast-riding horseman arrived with a message from Batang. It was the long-expected communication from the Chinese Communists, but it was much worse than even the Pangdatshangs had anticipated.

In it the Chinese declared that they had already broadcast an agreement as having been settled in anticipation of the Pangdatshangs' and the Amdo leaders' compliance. The East Tibetan leaders were not to think that this was just another Chinese invasion to put down intransigent chieftains and establish political links with Lhasa. This was to be a much greater programme, for it was part of Communism's intention to liberate Asia and the world. The whole of Tibet was to be brought under Chinese Communist control, within the next year, and this would be followed by Nepal, Sikkim and Bhutan in three years, and then India in five years. They knew of the Kham and Amdo leaders' plans for revolt against the Lhasa Government, and approved of them, but instead of going ahead with them as a Tibetan partisan affair they should declare a rebellion against the reactionary feudal régime in Lhasa, and China would help them.

The Pangdatshangs were stunned at the implications of such a proposal, for it meant that instead of being a nationalist reform group they would have to be traitors fighting for the Chinese against their own countrymen. It was no use sending to Lhasa to inform the officials there of what was happening and to plead for help, for it was already known there that there were plans for revolt in East Tibet and this would be suspected as a ruse. Further, such a mission would take more than six months by the normal route through Chamdo, and it was obvious from the Chinese Communist advance in West China and from their letter that they would attack within that time. There was only one possibility. Someone would have to get through on the little-known trail to Sadiya in Assam which, by travelling almost night and day, might be done inside two months. In this way the news could be given to India or Britain, and then they could offer to help and bring pressure to bear on the Lhasa Government. If all agreed, word could be sent to East Tibet in time for them to make a stand against the Chinese.

But who was to take the message? Topgyay was required to stay in Kham as the recognized military leader of the Khambas; Rapga could not go to India, for the order of expulsion was still in effect against him and he might be arrested on arrival before he could do anything; others who could go were either not *au fait* with the whole situation or not in a position to approach ⊍fficials in India. I was the only one who filled all the conditions required, and I agreed to go.

I arrived in India within the two months and immediately approached the authorities. They were receptive but sceptical, and as Britain only had a *chargé d'affaires* in Peking, and the U.S. no one at all, it was left to India to find out through her ambassador in Peking, Sardar Pannikar, just how true my information was. Unfortunately, Sardar Pannikar was persuaded that it was untrue, that any movements of troops in West China were only normal precautions to protect their frontier against western aggression, and that China had more than enough to keep her occupied internally for the next ten years.

This was communicated to the Lhasa Government, and I also sent word to the Pangdatshangs by special messenger. I had been delayed much longer than had been anticipated and before I could return, first the monsoons broke, then a violent earthquake occurred, and finally an illness in hospital prevented me from returning in time.

It had been decided by the Kham and Amdo leaders before I left East Tibet that in the event of my death on the way, or some unavoidable inability to return, or failing any help from the outside powers or the Lhasa Government, the East Tibetan leaders would co-operate to some extent with the Chinese in their plans. They would not agree to march against Lhasa, but would co-operate in other ways to keep power in their hands as long as possible. This the Chinese would definitely require, because the racial antagonism of the Khambas for the Chinese would necessitate using Tibetans in leading positions for some time. Topgyay thought that they might be able to hold power for ten years, but Rapga, more informed and realistic, thought five years at the most. If during that time the Lhasa Government, or the outside powers, decided to fight the Chinese in Tibet, word should be sent to them. They would then pass the message on to the many chieftains in East Tibet, and revolt from the inside.

The advance units of the Communist army arrived in the Pangdatshang valley of Bo in August 1950. They brought with them certain offers to the Pangdatshangs, including a Ten-Point Agreement which they requested Rapga to take to Chamdo as an emissary to the Lhasa Government. He reached Chamdo one day before Ngabu Shape, the new Governor, arrived to take over from Lhalu, the retiring Governor. The Chamdo appointment, as Governor of Kham under the Lhasa Government, was considered as banishment into the Tibetan wilderness, for there was no social life and no possibility of self-advancement by intrigue or otherwise. Ngabu had been considered a *parvenu* in Lhasa, and something of a political nuisance, for he had been constantly trying to urge reform in the cabinet and Kashag. The routine reappoint-

E   65

ment for Chamdo coming up, it was thought a good move in Lhasa to put Ngabu there and so remove a source of trouble to themselves.

When Ngabu arrived he found that Lhalu wanted to reject the Chinese overtures and to fight, but Ngabu maintained that support from the Lhasa Government would not be forthcoming and that resistance in these circumstances was out of the question; in addition, the gap between the local Kham people and the Government officials was too great and with the strong feeling against Lhasa they could expect little support from them. His opinion was confirmed after they wirelessed Lhasa, and the Government ordered them to take no action as they were going to talk to the Chinese Communists through New Delhi.

On being informed of the Lhasa decision Rapga suggested to Ngabu and Lhalu his plans for the reform of the Lhasa Government and the establishment of a new Representative Government covering the whole of Greater Tibet. This newly formed and declared Popular Government would then send a rejection to the Chinese Communists. For this the Khambas would fight but for nothing less. The new Governor took a draft copy of the plan to study and he tentatively agreed, but before anything could be done the Chinese attacked on October 29, 1950.

They struck from the north through Jyekundo, Derge and Gangto Druga, from the east through Kangting and Batang, and from the south through Atuntze and Tsakalo. With the Khambas held in check by the Pangdatshangs the Tibetan Army had no chance at all, and except for the deaths of about four hundred Khambas, who could not resist joining in the fighting, there were few other casualties. Ngabu, Lhalu and Robert Ford, the British wireless operator working for the Tibetan Government in Chamdo, escaped but were captured by a Chinese flanking movement and brought back to Chamdo.

The Chinese presented Ngabu and Lhalu with the ultimatum of agreeing to their Ten-Point Agreement or facing all-out war. When the ultimatum was forwarded to Lhasa, the Government agreed to negotiate, appointing Rapga and a Chinese-speaking Tibetan official, Yishe-Dargyay, son of the Foreign Minister, to talk over the terms. On Rapga's credentials as negotiator the naïve Lhasa Government had inserted instructions that he must only concede permission for the Chinese to enter Tibet when everything else had failed and that even then he should insist that the occupation of Tibet should be temporary and viewed as a concession during the period of China's declared fear of external aggression through Tibet. This is the reason the Chinese gave at the time for moving into Tibet. They did not claim then, as they did later, that it was part of their own territory.

As the talks dragged on the Chinese finally demanded that another delegation be sent to Peking. Ngabu was appointed leader, with some officials from Kham, and some from Lhasa to travel via India to China. From that time Ngabu was brought under strict observation and not allowed to talk to another Tibetan without a Chinese being present.

To the north-east, in Amdo, the Chinese were also infiltrating into Tibet, trying if possible to avoid a major clash of arms which might have created international interest. The Panchen Lama sent a telegram from Chinghai to Mao Tse-tung and the Commander-in-Chief of the People's Army, Chu Teh, to express his support for the 'liberation' of Tibet and to invite the Chinese Government's co-operation in introducing reforms into his country.

In India the members of a Tibetan Government delegation who had been on their way to China for discussions before the attack on Tibet, again under the leadership of Shakabpa, were held up in India because, they claimed, Britain would not issue them with travel visas for Hong Kong. When the Chinese Communists attacked Tibet this delegation forwarded an appeal to the United Nations, dated November 7, 1950, which, although raised by the El Salvador delegate, was repressed at the request of the Jam Sahib of Nawanagar, India's delegate. Tibetans felt this action was at the instigation of Krishna Menon.

India did try to protest to China in notes through its ambassador in Peking, but weakly, simply pointing out its concern and the possible effect such an action might have on China's entering the United Nations. To the communication the Peking Government brusquely replied:

'Tibet is an integral part of Chinese territory, and the Tibetan problem is entirely the domestic problem of China. . . . Regardless of whether the local authorities wish to proceed with peace negotiations and whatever the results of such negotiations, no interference whatsoever from a foreign country will be tolerated.'

In the Indian note, categorically denying the Chinese charges of foreign-influenced decisions, the Government stressed the fact of Tibetan autonomy and reiterated its plea for a peaceful settlement of the Tibetan issue.

The Tibetan delegation in Kalimpong sent a cablegram to the United Nations on November 28 to urge the immediate discussion of its appeal, and followed it on December 8 with another expressing 'surprise and regret' but all to no effect.

In Lhasa there was not only the same surprise, regret, agony and despair but a situation verging on the panic-stricken. Many officials and leading families left the capital for Kalimpong in India, taking families and wealth with them. The Regent and Government, under pressure of events, decided to let the seventeen-year-old Dalai Lama assume his majority before the normal time and on December 17 he was installed as Dalai Lama with full temporal and religious power.

On May 23, 1951, the Tibetan delegation led by Ngabu, although not authorized to do more than discuss the new situation with China, was forced to sign a Seventeen-Point Agreement in Peking. On September 9, 1951, the Chinese Army entered Lhasa for the fourth time.

But this time there was a difference; for this was a more ominous invasion than the others in that the Chinese were the declared bearers of a mission to 'liberate' Asia and the world.

Part Two

CAUSES OF REVOLT

CHAPTER 7

Kalimpong—'Nest of Spies'

W̲hat Kangting is on the Sino-Tibetan trade route Kalimpong is on the Indo-Tibetan. The border town terminus of the Central Asian trade routes, it is one of the most colourful and charming towns in India.

The road into Kalimpong, after running beside the foaming River Teesta in the steep, tree-lined valley, rises dramatically in a series of sweeping bends, climbing the mountain-face for nine miles. Where the dark green of the trees thins out the light green of paddy and maize fields in geometric terraces takes over. Flaming scarlet rhododendrons and bougainvilleas follow the delicate blue of jacaranda and pink of cherry or the exotically scented 'lady of the night'.

From the seventh milestone from the Teesta Valley bridge the town begins to unfold. At first there are small, mud-walled, straw-thatched *bustees*, or clusters of houses, often completely hidden by the tall-growing maize, then from the eighth mile wooden or lath-and-plaster houses with corrugated-iron roofs begin to take over. From here to the eleventh mile is the town of Kalimpong proper. The areas of the town are delineated by the milestones, or, to be more exact, the half-mile stones which mark the side of the road through the town and on to Pedong beyond.

The town is scattered along a ridge lying at an elevation of 3,933 feet to 4,650 feet, with the bazaar in the seat of the saddle, and with the two sentinel points of Durbindara, 4,500 feet, and Deolo, 5,590 feet, on either side. The mountain drops away sharply on each side of the ridge, giving an unobstructed and unparalleled view of the Himalayas and the three countries of Nepal,

71

Sikkim and Bhutan. Towering above all is the 28,146-foot Kanchenjunga massif with four other peaks all over 20,000 feet, and at least six others over the 15,000-foot mark. From Durbindara on a clear day over two hundred miles of mountain peaks are visible in what must be one of the most breathtaking views to be seen anywhere in the world.

The town is divided into five areas, starting at the north on Deolo hill with Dr. Graham's Homes for Anglo-Indian children; then the 'eleventh mile' area of Tibetan caravanserais; the 'tenth mile' of Tibetan and Chinese shops; the bazaar itself; and, finally, the 'Development Area'—the district laid out in the last days of the British régime in India, with large European-style houses and lovely gardens.

The population of Kalimpong varies a great deal as there are over five thousand Tibetans who come and go during a normal trading season, but a recent figure was 11,961, this including the Homes, Scots Mission and Development Area. It is the population of Kalimpong which constitutes one of its greatest attractions. On a market day there may be seen Nepalese, Bengalis, Sikkimese, Bhutanese, Lepchas, Chinese, Mongolians, Tibetans, Mohammedans, Marwaris and other Indian nationals, not to mention the great variety of Europeans who are annually drawn to this charming Himalayan town. Except for occasional tension between Nepalese and Bengalis there is a wonderful spirit of friendship and hospitality between all communities.

As befits a border town and terminus of an important trade route, the main occupation of Kalimpong is trade. During the trading season, when the passes into Tibet are open, the main street of Kalimpong is packed with trucks, bullock carts, mules, horses and coolies all engaged in the transport of goods to and from shops and godowns. In the shops the tall, swash-buckling Tibetan muleteers, or the more elegant traders, haggle good-naturedly over the prices quoted by the Indian merchants or Chinese leather-makers.

Each morning long caravans of red-plumed mules, bells jingling, bringing bales of Tibetan yak wool and musk, enter Kalimpong, passing equally long caravans leaving Kalimpong with cloth, tea, cigarettes, kerosene, sugar, food grains and some luxury items on the six-month journey to Lhasa and China.

It was down this route from Lhasa that the Dalai Lama and leading members of his Government fled in 1951 when the Chinese Communists occupied Lhasa.

I had rented a house in the new Development Area of Kalimpong in 1950, when it was impossible for me to return to Tibet. Within a few months I had for my neighbours the leading members of the Lhasa Government and Tibetan aristocracy. The Dalai Lama's mother and sister were only two houses away, Surkhang, one of the Cabinet ministers, was next door, Shakabpa, the Finance Minister and leader of the Trade Delegation, only a few hundred yards away, and so on throughout the area wherever houses were available.

This influx of a hitherto remote people, inaccessible behind their mountain barriers and political obstacles, at the same time as the dramatic and unexpected attack on Tibet by the Chinese, brought newspaper correspondents, tourists, scholars and other, more ambiguous, figures into Kalimpong from all over the world.

It was a peculiar and unprecedented situation for the Press and that perhaps accounted for the misrepresentation of what was happening in Tibet which went on in even the most responsible newspapers. The Tibetans were not publicity-conscious and, in any case, had been taken so completely by surprise by the Chinese attack (after the assurances which had been given them to the contrary) that they were in no position to talk even had they so wished. Very few of them spoke English and no correspondent who obtained an interview could speak Tibetan, so that they were thrown on the unsatisfactory expedient of collecting information in the bazaar from muleteers and others through bilingual locals. By the time the Tibetan officials realized the damage that was being done in the world's Press by imaginative reporting, and had protested, the crisis had passed, editors had ceased to be interested, and complaints received no publicity. The picture of Tibet which had been given to the world was a combination of James Hilton's *Lost Horizon*, Lobsang Rampa's *The Third Eye* and Harrer's *Seven Years in Tibet*—simple prayer-muttering people, with a

Gilbert-and-Sullivan army, armed with antique, muzzle-loading rifles, and a superstitious priesthood, fleeing in terror before the disciplined formations of the Chinese Army. One report even had it that the Dalai Lama fled because of a superstitious prognostication involving some balls of tsamba.

In Kalimpong confusion was worse confounded by the Tibetans themselves indulging in the feudal intrigues between the various families and groups. Shakabpa, who had been the leader of the earlier Trade Delegation and was now the leader of the proposed Delegation waiting to proceed to Peking, was a protégé of Tagta Rimpoche, the usurper of the Regency who had ordered the death of Reting, and as such was bitterly disliked by the pro-Reting elements; also he was anti-Ngabu, and all his recommendations to the Lhasa Government were directed towards diminishing Ngabu's possible influence from East Tibet. Further, I had learned from Yangpel Pangdatshang that Shakabpa, for reasons of his own, had not communicated to the Lhasa Government my messages from Topgyay and Rapga Pangdatshang as to the danger of approaching Chinese Communism and their request for instructions to fight. I saw quite a bit of Shakabpa at this time and came to like him very much as a person while disagreeing completely with his policies. For four months I lived in the same house with two members of the pro-Shakabpa faction, Shudrun Lobsang Yeshi and Dreyul; the former was later to play a heroic role in the revolt in Lhasa and escape of the Dalai Lama, and the latter to go completely Communist.

Then there were the cross-currents of confusion caused by those whose interests were either pro-Dalai Lama or pro-Panchen Lama, the latter a minority but vocal nevertheless; and the various aristocratic families jockeying for prestige and power in a set of circumstances introduced by Communist occupation of which they knew nothing at all.

The priests added their own quota to it all by digging out ancient prophecies, from the one foretelling that deliverance and prosperity would come to Tibet from Shambala—the mythical Tibetan 'Paradise' believed to be situated somewhere to the north of Tibet—to the doomed one foretelling that there would never be a Fourteenth Dalai Lama, that the incarnation would cease with the Thirteenth. To those who sought to argue that there was a Fourteenth Dalai Lama living the gloomy would point out that he had only been installed as Dalai Lama after the Chinese had arrived in Tibet, that he had only been sixteen when installed on November 17, 1950, two years earlier than was usual for a Dalai Lama, that he had never ruled as Dalai Lama, and that he had fled from Lhasa shortly after his installation to Yatung on the Indian border.

Yatung was only a good day-and-a-half by horse from Kalimpong. From Kalimpong to Gangtok, the capital of Sikkim, was forty-six miles, and could be traversed in four hours by car, but from just beyond Gangtok the road ceased and the next thirty miles had to be done on horseback.

In February 1951 the Tibetan Government, scattered in Lhasa, Yatung and Kalimpong, agreed at the direction of the new young Dalai Lama to despatch a fresh delegation to Peking under the leadership of Ngabu, at that time in Chamdo in East Tibet. In addition to those who would accompany him through East Tibet and West China to Peking, two others, Khemoy Sonam Wangdi and Thupten Tenthor, came from Yatung through Kalimpong and Calcutta to join them in Peking. None of the earlier delegates under the leadership of Shakabpa was included. The instructions given to the delegation were to hold exploratory talks only; they were not authorized to sign any agreement on behalf of the Dalai Lama or the Tibetan Government.

All this time the Chinese Army remained in Chamdo in East Tibet, making no attempt to move farther into Tibet. At the same time, in response to the protests which had arisen in India against China's armed aggression in Tibet, the Chinese launched a virulent attack on India, accusing the Indians of being 'the running dogs of imperialism'.

More than any other single person the Indian Ambassador to Peking, Sardar K. M. Pannikar, was responsible for the loss of Tibet and the unpreparedness of India to meet the situation. In reply to the information which I had brought from East Tibet that the Chinese were about to attack Tibet in a programme of expansion to take over Nepal, Sikkim, Bhutan and India, he had said that this was nonsense, that any movements of troops on China's borders with Tibet were only to safeguard China's frontiers against Western aggression, and that the Chinese Government had enough to keep it occupied in China for the next ten or twenty years.

In his book *In Two Chinas*, Sardar Pannikar writes: 'To add to my trouble, by the middle of the month, rumours of a Chinese invasion of Tibet began to circulate. Visits and representations to the Foreign Office brought no results. The Wai Chiapu officials were polite but silent. Things were certainly moving on that side. The only information I was able to wring out of them was that certain precautionary measures were being taken in West Sikang, that is on the borders of Tibet proper. In India, mainly as a result of messages from American and Hong Kong correspondents, public opinion was already excited. On the 25th of October, however, the Chinese announced on the Peking Radio that the process of "Liberating Tibet" had begun. The fat was in the fire. The Government of India was troubled about the Chinese action on the Tibetan border and I received instructions to lodge a strong protest. The Chinese reply was equally strong. It practically accused India of having been influenced by the imperialists, and claimed that China had not taken any military action, but was determined to liberate Tibet by peaceful means. . . .

'I had expected a virulent campaign against India in the Press. But for some reason the Chinese, apart from publishing the correspondence, soft-pedalled the whole affair. The controversy was seldom mentioned in the Press. But on our side matters were not so easy. The Indian Press, egged on by the sensational reports of the American correspondents and the blood-curdling stories issued from Hong Kong by Taipeh agents, kept on talking about Chinese aggression. Even Sardar Patel, the Deputy Prime Minister, felt called upon to make an unfriendly speech. There was also some support in the External Affairs Ministry for the view that India should act vigorously to protect Tibet. . . . Knowing the temper of the Indian public and the attitude of some of the officials I was nervous that the Government might take some hasty step. . . .'

Then later, 'The Tibetan question had also settled itself, for the Chinese after the first military display were content to keep their armies on the frontier and await the arrival of the Tibetan delegation for a settlement by negotiations. . . .'

Pannikar's almost audible sigh of relief at the successful *fait accompli* of the Chinese, coupled with Krishna Menon's efforts to have the Tibetan appeal to the United Nations shelved, found no echo in the hearts of Tibetans inside Tibet or in Kalimpong. Kalimpong became a hive of activity as various Tibetan officials either openly or secretly made contact with Indians, British and Americans in their attempts to find help.

Kungo Liusha, a Cabinet Minister, was sent to Kalimpong to see if he could resolve the dispute between Tibet and India regarding the bonding of Tibetan wool through India without tax, which the Tibetans claimed India was doing and thereby violating the Geneva Convention which gave any inland country a right to the sea. This appropriation of tax, plus the fact that the Tibetans were not being allowed to use the dollars accumulating from their wool trade with the U.S. but had to apply to the India Reserve Bank for permission to use them, increased the growing animosity of the Tibetans towards the Indian Government. The situation was not helped by the supercilious and off-hand treatment accorded to the Tibetan representatives by the local Indian Political Officer at the time.

Then the whole question of Tibetan trade hung in the balance, for with the occupation by China the U.S. had sent their Economic Attaché to Kalimpong to inform Liusha and Yangpel Pangdatshang, who were conducting the trade talks, that the U.S. were considering stopping all wool trade with Tibet in accordance with the U.S. policy of not trading with any Communist country or its satellite. As eighty per cent of Tibetan wool was sent to America this was a crippling blow to the Tibetans, who now faced economic disaster and a complete handing over of their country to the advancing Chinese.

The Russians were also busy throughout this period, making separate approaches to the Tibetans through their intelligence agent in Kalimpong. While he was a well-known figure, and apparently beyond reproach, it was amusing to know, almost as soon as he had made his proposals on Russia's behalf, just what these proposals were. The Tibetan officials were so baffled by the spectacle of China and Russia working at cross-purposes that they consulted me on the proposals, and their possible significance, shortly after they had been approached by the Russian agent. Broadly speaking, the Russian attitude seemed to be that while they preferred a Communist occupation of Tibet to a 'feudal' or 'imperialist' one, both Russia and China were suspicious of each other's possible growing influence in High Asia and both were out to shift the balance of power in their own favour, China openly and Russia by more subtle methods.

On May 23, to the surprise and consternation of the Dalai Lama and members of the Tibetan Government, Peking announced that the delegation which had been sent for exploratory talks had signed an agreement between Tibet and China, called the Seventeen-Point Agreement. This declared that 'the Tibetan people shall unite and drive out imperialist aggressive forces from Tibet and shall return to the big family of the Motherland—the People's Republic of China'. The Agreement went on to promise the maintenance of the *status quo* in the Tibetan regional government structure as well as in the internal position and authority of the Dalai Lama but called on the Lhasa Government actively to assist the People's Liberation Army to enter Tibet and consolidate the national defences, while permitting 'autonomy under the unified leadership of the Central People's Government'. Tibetan troops were to be reorganized into the People's Liberation Army, and all foreign affairs to be handled by Peking. To ensure that the Agreement was implemented the Central People's Government would establish in Tibet a military and administrative committee, and a military area headquarters with as many Tibetans as could be absorbed.

Tibetan officials in Kalimpong and Yatung were overwhelmed by this development, for no one had authorized the delegation to sign an agreement, and no preparation had been made for the event.

While controversy raged over what should be the next step to

take in repudiating this imposed Agreement, in view of the fact
that the U.N. had evinced no interest and India had committed
herself to non-intervention and even connivance, the Dalai
Lama's eldest brother, Taktser Rimpoche, slipped quietly into
Kalimpong.

CHAPTER 8

The Dalai Lama and the U.S.

I met Taktser Rimpoche, at the invitation of Yangpel Pangdat-shang, in the house of his mother and sister, who were near neighbours of mine. It was an ordinary tea party, with the usual exchange of courtesies, but that same evening he called on me at my home to discuss more momentous matters. He had brought with him several armed guards and these he stationed outside the house as we talked.

It transpired that he had been in East Tibet, an incarnate lama in the great Kumbum Monastery, when the Chinese attacked in 1950. He had been captured by the Chinese and after a short respite had been invited to proceed to China. While there he had gradually been persuaded to 'reform his thinking' and accept in some measure the Communist indoctrination. He had not been convinced, but had co-operated with the Chinese as there was no other hopeful course open to him. After some time the Chinese had approached him with the suggestion that he co-operate with them in taking over Tibet.

The People's Liberation Army was still in Chamdo and had not advanced farther. His part would be to return to Lhasa ahead of the army with a Chinese diplomatic delegation. On arriving in Lhasa he would persuade the Lhasa Government that it was useless to resist, and he would seek their co-operation in inviting the Chinese Army to Lhasa and submitting to China. In time he would depose the Dalai Lama, and in return for his collaboration the Chinese would appoint him as President in Tibet in the Dalai Lama's place.

Taktser Rimpoche had no option but to agree, and left Chamdo with a five member delegation for Lhasa. Shortly before reaching Lhasa, on the pretext that it was customary to send a message ahead to announce their imminent arrival, he sent a message with his trusted servant that the approaching delegation was a ruse in the Chinese plan to take over Tibet, and that the Dalai Lama and the Cabinet should flee. Unfortunately the servant had not been believed and the Dalai Lama and his ministers were still in Lhasa when Taktser Rimpoche and the delegation arrived.

However, when Taktser Rimpoche had had a private talk with the Dalai Lama and the members of the Kashag they believed him, and it was this information and not any superstitious mumbo-jumbo which had caused the Dalai Lama's precipitate departure from Lhasa to Yatung.

He, Taktser, had come with the Dalai Lama. When the news of the flight had reached the Chinese they had immediately ordered his death before he could divulge any more of the Chinese intentions to the outside world. He had stopped in Yatung for some time, but now that the Chinese were about to move into Lhasa and West Tibet he had to escape before they could capture him or before some pro-Communist Tibetan or Indian could kill him.

He had brought with him two letters from the Dalai Lama, one a personal letter requesting those whom it concerned to provide whatever help Taktser Rimpoche required; the other authorizing Taktser Rimpoche to speak on behalf of the Dalai Lama and conclude an agreement with any outside power which would help Tibet and also make arrangements for the Dalai Lama's escape. The letters and their intentions were known only to Taktser Rimpoche, the Dalai Lama, and Trichang Rimpoche, the tutor to the Dalai Lama. Taktser had arranged to communicate with the Dalai Lama through Trichang Rimpoche by a secret code known only to the three of them. He, Taktser, wanted to escape to America and he said that it was with America that the Dalai Lama wished to make a secret agreement.

I went ahead to Calcutta to make arrangements for his escape to America. He was afraid to move out of Kalimpong too soon, as to do so would give the Chinese or other Communists some indication of his plans. Even his mother and sister had no knowledge of his intentions. When all arrangements possible without his presence had been made I sent for him to come to Calcutta for the final discussions. After talks with U.S. representatives and several cabled conversations with Delhi and Washington a preliminary agreement was drawn up to be communicated to the Dalai Lama. Briefly the terms were:

1. On his escaping from Tibet the U.S. would agree to support the Dalai Lama and one hundred and twenty members of his government for an indefinite period in any country of the Dalai Lama's choosing, but it was thought advisable that the country should be in the East.

2. The U.S. would take up the matter of China's aggression against Tibet, and Tibet's plea for help, in the U.N.

3. The U.S. would provide finance for whatever was required in Tibet's fight for freedom from the Chinese.

4. Any question of military assistance would have to be left for future discussions, but on his arrival in India the Dalai Lama should approach the Indian Government for help, and when this was refused, as it would be, he was to request the Indian Government for permission to approach any other country willing to help.

The provisions in the agreement were conditional upon one action by the Dalai Lama. Before leaving Tibet he should repudiate the Seventeen-Point Agreement just signed by the Tibetan delegation in Peking, and immediately on his arrival in India he should again publicly repudiate it.

The terms of the agreement having been sent to Yatung, together with the information about arrangements for the Dalai Lama's reception in India, Taktser Rimpoche was free to leave for the U.S. at any time.

However, the news of his arrival in Calcutta had reached the Chinese. As the discussions went on the Chinese grew suspicious and acted swiftly to counteract any possible action. At first we were only followed wherever we went, but in a few days the Chinese Advisory Delegation, under the leadership of Chang Ching-wu, flew from Peking to Calcutta with some of the members of the Tibetan delegation. Immediately on their arrival in

Calcutta they attempted to make contact with Taktser Rimpoche. He refused to see any visitors, even Tibetans, on the plea that he was unwell, but the Chinese finally sent his brother-in-law, who had been a member of the Tibetan delegation, to visit him. Taktser Rimpoche had to see him, but he kept to his story that he was unwell and unable to see Chang Ching-wu as his brother-in-law suggested.

Finally the Chinese Ambassador came from New Delhi to Calcutta, ostensibly to meet the members of the Advisory Delegation but actually to bring more pressure on Taktser Rimpoche. He peremptorily sent a message to Taktser Rimpoche to say that if he would not call to see them at the Chinese Consulate, they would call on him at the hotel where he was staying.

Even then Taktser Rimpoche was reluctant to go, but he was finally persuaded to pay a short visit on the assurance that he would be carefully watched and guarded by Indian Security police. After being harangued by the Chinese Ambassador for his activities and being promised forgiveness for his past defections, he agreed with the Ambassador's directions that he should leave India. He left the Consulate on this promise. While the Ambassador thought he meant for Tibet and China, Taktser Rimpoche had meant—deliberately—the U.S.

While he slipped away quietly to the U.S. the Chinese Advisory Delegation left for Kalimpong and Tibet in the assurance that there was no further danger from that quarter. They were still in Kalimpong when a few days later the news was announced in the world's press that Taktser Rimpoche had arrived in New York. The news threw Kalimpong into a ferment of expectation. Had Taktser Rimpoche gone to America for help? Was America going to send troops to help Tibet? Was the Dalai Lama about to come to India?

If Kalimpong was gripped in a fever of controversy it was nothing to what was happening in the Chinese camp. The Chinese Advisory Delegation to Tibet was stranded in Kalimpong, not knowing whether to proceed or to return to Calcutta, New Delhi or Peking. The longer they hesitated in Kalimpong the more face they lost, but they dared not proceed to Yatung lest the Dalai

Lama and the Kashag should leave for India and no one would be there when they arrived. They too, were faced by the possibility of American help in some form being sent to Tibet, and a whole new set of circumstances arising from this possibility.

To make matters even more tense, the editor of the only Tibetan newspaper, the *Tibet Mirror*, published in Kalimpong, had received several pages of typed foolscap with details of briefing for the use of American troops in Tibet and had been asked to publish it in his newspaper. Fortunately he was perturbed and he consulted some officials. On their advice he did not publish, but the information was not secret and had been passed round, thereby heightening the expectation.

When Taktser Rimpoche had left India all arrangements had been made for the Dalai Lama to leave Yatung in six days, that is, on July 12, 1951. Assurance had already been received from the Indian Prime Minister, Mr. Nehru, that he would be given sanctuary in India should he so desire. The only difficulty remaining was the method of escape. He still did not know whom to trust in his immediate entourage, for many high officials had accepted the Chinese assurances that they would not interfere with Tibetan customs or privileges. Yangpel Pangdatshang had agreed to provide two hundred armed Khambas to bring the Dalai Lama to safety, on condition that the Dalai Lama personally requested him to do so; he would not trust any other person in the Lhasa Government.

Three days later I received a letter from the Dalai Lama, through his brother-in-law who had taken my letter to the Dalai Lama, to say that he would have to return to Lhasa. The three abbots of the three great monasteries in Lhasa, Sera, Drepung and Ganden, had arrived in Yatung from Lhasa, and suspecting that the Dalai Lama might be contemplating leaving for India, they had insisted that he consult the State Oracle. The Dalai Lama had submitted to this and the State Oracle, under possession, had advised him to return to Lhasa. The Dalai Lama had been unwilling to accept this, and had defied precedent by demanding a second possession. Again the State Oracle had decreed that he should return to Lhasa. When the Dalai Lama had been going to refuse this direction as well, the three abbots had said: 'If you do not accept the direction of the gods on high, how can you expect to be accepted as their representative on earth?' and he had had to submit. Nevertheless, he sent his thanks for what had been done, and undertook to keep in mind all that had been sent to him and to use it when a suitable opportunity arose.

On July 16 the Dalai Lama and members of his Government in Yatung had a meeting with Chang Ching-wu to discuss his return to Lhasa, and on July 21 he left Yatung on his return journey.

On September 9 the People's Liberation Army entered Lhasa. On March 13, 1952, they entered Yatung and were deployed along the northern frontier of Bhutan and Assam. On April 28, escorted by Chinese troops, the Panchen Lama arrived in Lhasa, and what the Chinese had declared to be 'the Peaceful Liberation of Tibet' was complete.

CHAPTER 9

Opposition to Chinese Development

On entering Tibet the Chinese Army was in a sorry condition and in no physical state to have withstood strong Tibetan opposition. Not only the Tibetans but observers such as Robert Ford and Geoffrey Bull have recorded that the advance units of the Chinese Army straggled into the various towns and villages in the desolate plateaux tattered, insufficiently clothed, underfed and exhausted. The several months of marking time in Chamdo helped them to recuperate from the gruelling marches at fifteen thousand feet altitudes, and they were put to the task of building the road which was to be the main trade route through Tibet.

However, had it been left to the Chinese alone the road never would have been built. They had the engineers, they had some of the labour in the ranks of the Occupation Army, but they were not physically equipped to work at such heights where the slightest exertion brought on an extreme vertigo to all except Tibetans. Consequently they recruited Tibetans for the work of clearing the trails of stones, building up the narrow parts and draining the muddy sections where the coming transport might break down. They even went so far as to pay the high wages to the Tibetans in the Chinese silver dollar, and not in paper currency which the Tibetans distrusted after the late Kuomingtang fiasco in China.

There was no attempt at providing a network of roads to facilitate administration, but all efforts were concentrated on building, widening and bridging the two main trails converging on Chamdo, the one from the north at Sining through Jyekundo, and the other from the east at Kangting through Kantze; from Chamdo they joined in one road to Lhasa. Those were the trails

86

followed by centuries of caravans of yaks and mules from India to China, and in many places they required little more than clearing away the stones from the bare plateaux. But the building of over a hundred bridges and the shoring up of high, narrow trails across the face of precipitous mountains was a major engineering feat.

As the Liberation Army advanced from Chamdo through Riwoche and Gyamda Dzong to Lhasa, they left behind garrisons every five miles to maintain the road and guard their supply lines into Tibet; for food was their major problem. Most of Tibet being at an unproductive altitude of fifteen thousand feet, the amount of food produced by the farming section of the country was scarcely sufficient to feed the Tibetans and to leave some over for storage in granaries. Barley, the staple food of the Tibetans, was grown up to a height of seven thousand feet, and in South Tibet rice was grown up to about four thousand feet, but extra supplies of both barley and rice, particularly the latter, had to be bought from lower-lying Bhutan. Notwithstanding, in all my travels in Tibet, admittedly mostly amongst the Khambas of the east, I never saw a hungry Tibetan. Certainly there were beggars, and in some places many of them, but they were all well-fed and were beggars in the religiously mendicant sense of providing the means whereby the giver could obtain virtue by donating food and alms.

With the influx of the fifty-thousand People's Liberation Army it became of the utmost importance to the Chinese to see that their supplies were adequate so that their presence in Tibet did not upset this precariously maintained balance. In any case, the tsamba (barley flour) and dried meat which the Tibetans found adequate as their staple diet did not appeal to the rice- and vege-table-eating Chinese. At one time in 1952, shortly after their occu-pation of the country, it looked as if they might have drastically to cut down their Occupation Army, or even withdraw, as their food supplies were so low that there was wide discontent amongst the troops. Ironically they were able to survive this crisis by making an offer of rice to famine-stricken India and attaching as part-condition that several thousand maunds of the rice be sent to Tibet.

Opposition to Chinese Development

Farm implements, agricultural loans and technical experts on farming were sent to Tibet by the Peking Government in an enthusiastic attempt to overcome what they claimed was the reactionary feudal policy of the past, but with the exception of some few local successes, in the country as a whole the great agricultural experiment was not productive and the grim natural conditions of the highest country in the world defied their efforts.

In the towns and villages along their route of conquest the Chinese also built primary schools, medical and veterinary dispensaries and, in Chamdo and Lhasa, hospitals. They made school attendance compulsory for the Tibetan children during the day and for adults at night. Both the Tibetan and Chinese languages were taught in these schools, with hygiene, simple crafts, history, citizenship and politics.

The Liberation Army were scrupulous in their behaviour, keeping strictly to themselves and not oppressing the Tibetan populace in any way. Heavy penalties were imposed on any Chinese soldier who was known to have made use of even a Tibetan prostitute. One Chinese soldier, accused by a Tibetan woman of raping her, was shot by his superior officer.

With all the beneficent and necessary reforms being introduced one ominous factor emerged, that the innovations were not being made on a national scale but were limited strictly to the cities, towns and villages on the main route through Tibet to India. In effect, they were merely supplementary to the military thrust to the Indian border; there was no attempt to develop the country outside the main arteries.

Again, most of the beneficial reforms and the Chinese restraint had been limited to the showplaces of Lhasa and the towns west of Lhasa, where Indians were in residence and where this exemplary Chinese behaviour could be observed and reported. In East Tibet their approach was more often on the accepted Communist pattern.

After Taktser Rimpoche's defection and escape to America the Chinese had attacked Kumbum Monastery, his seat, in Amdo Province and confiscated all the wealth—grain, treasury and lands—as punishment. They then made this the excuse for widespread requisitioning of monastery lands in a programme of land reform, giving the lands back to the peasants and denouncing the lama landlords who had taken fifty per cent of their toil and earnings for centuries.

In Kham they launched a campaign to disarm the Khamba tribesmen, who until then had been allowed to carry on as they had been in the habit of doing. It might have been a necessary preliminary to the introduction of normal government into a tribal economy, but their high-handed approach to the touchily independent Khambas was all wrong, and the Khambas replied that the Manchus had tried to disarm them and failed, the Chinese Nationalists had tried to disarm them and failed, and if the Communists now wanted to make the attempt they should come and do so. Whether it was this unexpected intransigence after all their genuinely beneficent efforts, or the increasing demands of the war in Korea, or a combination of both, is difficult to say, but instead of a temporary diplomatic withdrawal to placate the still suspicious and antagonistic bulk of the Tibetan population the Chinese decided the time had come for sterner measures.

In Kham the East Tibetan People's Government had been formed with six Vice-Presidents, the four revolutionary leaders among them—Lobsang Tsewong, and Geshi Sherab Gyaltso of Amdo, and Topgyay and Rapga Pangdatshang of Kham. After the formation of the Government in Kham, all the Kham officials had for a year followed Rapga's advice to refuse to accept any payment from the Chinese, but under the increased Chinese pressure they were made to do so.

By the new Chinese Communist demands they were also compelled to pay more taxes, particularly in crops, wool and herds, for the 'Aid to Korea' fund until they were paying more taxes to the Chinese than they had ever done to the monasteries. Through the veterinary dispensaries the Communists had estimated the wealth of the people and when they did not voluntarily give their animals as taxes the Communists requisitioned them.

Discontent and unrest spread throughout the various tribes in Kham and Amdo and there were local uprisings against Chinese

89

officials and garrisons. These might have spread quickly into a major revolt, seriously embarrassing China—already fighting in Korea—but for the Kham and Amdo leaders in the East Tibetan People's Government, who persuaded them to wait for a more suitable opportunity when they could unite in an uprising that would be successful.

The discontent even spread to Lhasa. In May 1952 a petition from the Mi-mang Tsong-du (meaning 'People's Party', an organization which was anti-Chinese in emphasis but only functioning in Lhasa) was presented to the Chinese authorities, the gist of which was:

The upholder of religion in Tibet was still the Dalai Lama, and for this reason the Chinese should respect and maintain his authority.

In accordance with the 1951 Agreement all estates, property and other national institutions and rights should not be reformed.

It was admitted that between the Thirteenth and Fourteenth Dalai Lamas there was very little progress, but what reforms were required the Tibetans wanted to introduce themselves in their own way.

Because of the recent fighting, billeting of so many Chinese troops in the country, and bad weather, the crops had failed and there was grave danger of starvation. The Chinese should withdraw and leave the Tibetan Government to introduce the necessary measures to correct this; also, to reform the petty debts and tax system.

The Chinese had no right to interfere with the Tibetan Army as it had sought to do, nor with the other matters of defence.

Trade relations with the outside countries should be normalized to what they were prior to Chinese occupation, and this could only be accomplished if the Chinese withdrew.

Finally, Tibet wanted freedom according to international law.

However, many of the younger officials and sons of the aristocracy were enthusiastic about the Chinese reforms, for not only were they manifestly beneficial but they gave the young Tibetans something constructive to do for their country. This was something unknown in Tibet where official positions had been hereditary, class distinctions were rigid and unbridgeable, minor officials were seen and not heard, and government work had not been changed in centuries.

Many of the sons and daughters of the leading Tibetan families who had been studying in the colleges in Darjeeling were taken away under the new Chinese pressure and sent to study at the National Minorities University in Peking. Promising students from the newly instituted primary schools were also given scholarships to study in the more advanced schools and colleges in China. This also served the useful purpose of holding in check any tendency on the part of the parents to indulge in intrigue against China.

In a letter to me a friend in Kham, describing conditions since the Chinese occupation, wrote: 'In time, by sheer machine-like pressure, their propaganda resulted in many conversions to the dagger-and-smile policy of the Communists, and many succumbed to the promises of Utopia. However, it was not long until the Communists, despite their dazzling promises, began to cut down radically the payments being made to the higher officers. Those who stubbornly adhered to the policy of retaining the Buddhist religion, and the importance of Lhasa as a centre, were taken to China and subjected to "brain-washing". A few gave way under those methods and these were given responsible posts despite their inferior calibre. The intelligentsia, scholars and high-priests of the country were ridiculed and degraded. Individual liberty and free will were conspicuous by their absence. Dictated directions and instructions became the order of the day. Life had no meaning, no purpose. Willy-nilly, a person must part with his cattle, land, cereals, etcetera, whenever the Communists thought it necessary for their purpose. Taxes and tolls went up ten times more than in previous years. It is interesting to note that before the occupation by the Chinese régime, even in the most undeveloped and inaccessible part, butter was being sold at 25s. a maund and a sheep cost 45s. Now the situation is very different. Butter costs £7 and a sheep costs £30, and even at this price the things are scarce and unobtainable. Woe to the evil day that saw this holy land spoiled by such forces of misery. On top of all this, a constant

flow of arms still continues. Communication and transport are being introduced on a large scale. It is no doubt a good idea, but the
people have to groan under heavy taxation levied to pay for such
communications. There are signs of protests and exhaustion
everywhere. The mind and body are crushed beneath this callous
burden. . . .'

Early in 1953 a Tibetan from Amdo slipped quietly into Kalimpong. He was called Gompo Sham, and he was the son-in-law of
Lobsang Tsewong, one of the early revolutionary leaders and Vice-
President in the new East Tibetan People's Government. Like his
father-in-law Gompo Sham was a 'People's General' in the
Chinese-supervised Tibetan Army, and had been to China for
several periods of indoctrination. His story, like Taktser Rimpoche's, was a startling one.

He had travelled across Tibet from Amdo, disguised as a mendicant monk, in order to reach India with important information
and a message for Taktser Rimpoche. The Tibetans in Amdo
were now ready to revolt and they wanted Taktser Rimpoche's
assistance in approaching America for help.

It appeared that a crisis had been reached in Amdo where the
Chinese were exasperated by the non-co-operative attitude of the
Tibetans to their schemes of reform. Where the towns, villages
and monasteries were accessible the Chinese had been able to enforce their policies on the reluctant Tibetans, but in the remote
valleys and inaccessible mountains the Tibetans refused to submit
to the Chinese and in armed defiance carried on their lives as they
had always done.

When the Chinese sent in troops to coerce them into submission
the Amdo Tibetans, taking advantage of the mountainous terrain,
waited until the Chinese were deep in the mountains and then
attacked and killed them. The worst of all the fierce tribesmen in
this area, from the Chinese point of view, were the notorious
Goloks who had precipitated the crisis in Amdo and caused
Gompo Sham to leave immediately for India. The Chinese, exasperated by the continued defiance of the Goloks, had ordered Lobsang Tsewong and Gompo Sham to proceed to the Golok country
right away, with sufficient Chinese troops, to disarm the unruly

tribesmen and bring them under the control of the East Tibetan People's Government and China.

Like the Pangdatshangs in Kham, Lobsang Tsewong had hoped to keep power in his hands for some time by co-operating with the Chinese, but this crisis placed him in an impossible predicament. He knew that to go to the Goloks and ask them to hand over their arms and submit to China was to lose his prestige and leadership and virtually to commit suicide. On the other hand, to refuse to go would also mean certain death at the hands of the Chinese. He and Gompo Sham had therefore decided that now, sooner than they had anticipated, the time had come to call on the East Tibetan tribes to unite and fight the Chinese.

According to Gompo Sham, they were fairly well armed to fight for a short period of guerrilla warfare, but required much more equipment to be successful. They had been receiving occasional air-dropped supplies from Nationalist planes flying over Tibet from Formosa. When I expressed surprise at this he said that they had radios which had been brought by retreating Chinese Nationalist troops from the last days of the fighting in China.

He claimed that there were over eighty thousand rebels ready to fight in Amdo, not counting those in Kham. Amongst that number there were six thousand Chinese Nationalists formerly under the command of General Ma Bao-feng, and six thousand formerly under the command of General Ma Feng-kwei, who had retreated to Tibet before the advancing Chinese Communists and had settled amicably amongst the Amdo Tibetans in the mountains. The wireless operators were from amongst them.

Gompo Sham was disappointed on his arrival in Kalimpong to find that Taktser Rimpoche had gone to America, and he tried to obtain permission to visit him there. Apart from the normal difficulties of getting him a visa to go to America, and the problem of finding financial support for an indefinite period there, the Americans were in no position to take advantage of this new and valuable strategic possibility in Tibet. Any possible help for Tibet, military or otherwise, would have to pass through India, and it was a time of very poor relations between India and

America, due to Dulles's militant policies, Krishna Menon's attitude in the U.N., and the U.S. Congress's reluctance to send surplus grain to a famine-ridden India when Nehru was proving to be so obstinately anti-Western bloc.

Gompo Sham was advised by the U.S. authorities to go to Formosa and see what could be done there, but while arrangements were still being made the accumulating frustrations, and fears of failure and Chinese Communist reprisals, caused him to suffer a breakdown and he had to be admitted to a mental asylum for treatment.

However, even if nothing could be done, the information he had brought from Amdo about the feeling in East Tibet and the intentions of the leaders there was communicated to the Dalai Lama in Lhasa, who now knew that the majority of the Tibetan people inhabiting these areas were anti-Chinese and loyal to himself.

CHAPTER 10

China's Takeover Plans

Meanwhile, on the Indian border the Chinese military build-up began to look ominous. Military drill and army exercises were carried out from before dawn to dusk, and the constant stream of propaganda to the troops foretold the imminent invasion of Nepal, Sikkim and Bhutan. The Chinese border troops were so truculent that they arrested the Rani Chuni of Bhutan and her son, who were travelling from Bhutan across Tibet to India, and held them for several hours.

The propaganda and military activity on her borders at last began to worry India, and Mr. Nehru, with a large entourage of political and military advisers, made a personal tour of inspection of Kalimpong and Gangtok, in Sikkim. He was bluntly informed by his advisers that there was nothing India could do, either militarily or politically, to stop a Chinese invasion in the area. China's claim to the border states was based on the same assumptions as for Tibet.

In India headlines in the newspapers began to warn of the possibility of China's attack. 'We Are Next On Mao's List' read one, and Dr. Taraknath Das, a noted political commentator, wrote a warning article on the vulnerability of India's frontiers: 'If Sino-Russian forces move towards Northern India—especially North-Eastern India—India with her present relations with Pakistan, especially Eastern Pakistan where millions of Hindus are denied human rights, cannot defend herself. It is no secret (and the Government of India must have more adequate information than I have) that from Lhasa, as well as from Peking and Moscow, movements for cession of certain parts of North-Eastern India—

95

particularly Nepal, Bhutan, Sikkim and adjoining regions—and Chinese expansion into North Burma and Malaya are in full progress. . . .'

The *New York Times* also published an article, from information obtained on the spot, headed, 'Chinese Plan to Dominate Border States': 'Chinese Communists in Tibet plan to move 200,000 troops into the realm of the Living Buddha in order to dominate India's Himalayan border.

'In a long-range scheme Communist infiltration into Afghanistan, Nepal and Indian-protected States of Bhutan and Sikkim will be followed by penetration into India itself. Meanwhile the Communists have been unable to gain control over Tibet, except in the military sense. . . .'

In addition to the military preparations the Chinese had prepared a detailed intelligence programme of infiltration to accomplish their ambitions to 'liberate' the whole of Asia, details of which I was able to obtain from Kuomingtang intelligence agents in Kalimpong.

Citing the Seventeen-Point 1951 (the Sino-Tibetan) Agreement as their authority the Chinese officially merged the original Foreign Affairs Bureau of the Tibetan Government with the office of 'The Assistant-in-Charge of Foreign Affairs of the Central People's Government Representative in Tibet'. This in turn was linked with the 'Asiatic Section' of the International Communist Intelligence Bureau, with an impressive administration under the following seven offices:

1. Foreign Affairs Office
2. Border Affairs Office
   (a) Yatung Office
   (b) Lammo La Office
   (c) Tsona Office
   (d) Gartok Office, under Tihwa (Sinkiang) control
3. Training Academies
   (a) Staff Training Academy
   (b) Tibetan Languages Training Academy
   (c) Commercial (Traders) Training Academy

6. The author with Shrudrun Lobsang Yeshi, a Lhasa official, in Kalimpong in 1950. Shrudrun Lobsang Yeshi was a leader in the revolt in Lhasa and successfully organized the Dalai Lama's escape, but was killed when he returned to the city after seeing the Dalai Lama safely on his way

7. Rapga Pangdatshang, Khamba leader, with Robert Ford, radio operator in East Tibet at the time of the Chinese Communist 'liberation' in 1950

8. Part of a religious procession in Lhasa before the revolt

(d) Infiltrating Academy
1. India Infiltrating Class
2. Nepal Infiltrating Class
3. Bhutan and Sikkim Infiltrating Class
4. Espionage Office
(a) Transfer Section (Movement Control)
(b) Conference Section (Meetings, etc.)
5. Mines Research Office
6. Land Survey Office
7. Meteorological Office (Air and Climate Survey)

'Foreign Affairs' was under the control of the 'Advisory Bureau' and was directed from Peking through its head, Chang Ching-wu.

The 'Border Affairs Office' was concerned with intelligence related, as the name implies, to the border states of Bhutan, Nepal, Sikkim and India, and methods of infiltration into those areas. Yatung is a strategic point on the main trail from Tibet into Sikkim and India, and only about eighty miles from Kalimpong. Lamo La is on the Tibet-Nepal border, about eighty miles from Kathmandu, capital of Nepal. Tsona Dzong is a town on the border of Tibet and Bhutan, and directly adjoining India in Assam.

Members of the various intelligence and infiltration groups were taken mostly from bilingual border provinces between China and Tibet, such as Kham, Amdo, Yunnan, Kansu, and Sinkiang; they studied English, Hindi, Bengali, Nepali and Tibetan, as well as subsidiary intelligence activities, to further the Chinese plans for takeover in Asia, and the outlook of the border states and India looked bleak.

With almost three hundred thousand troops in Tibet the Chinese had to act quickly, either in advancing on the border states or in completely subjugating the whole of Tibet, for the country was agriculturally unfitted to support such an excess of population. What proved the undoing of the Chinese at the time was in attempting to do both.

They launched an intensive land reform campaign in East Tibet

G   97

which had as its real goal the elimination of the monasteries as centres of unrest. At the same time they used the recalcitrant monks and lay Tibetans as slave labour in a new drive to widen the roads for larger vehicular traffic.

A Khamba friend writing to me described conditions at the time:

'Their (the Chinese) greedy eyes are everywhere. The fair lands and all they contain do not escape their murderous purposes. Whether belonging to monk or layman, these lands are appropriated and in return a credit document is given. When the persons concerned claimed the value in money on the strength of the signed document or agreement, what happened? They were given an outright refutation accompanied by threats. They were snarled at, and told that the eaters of tsamba were the only persons clamouring for money. After all, they were not the only persons to be satisfied. There were many instances of persons who made such complaints being arrested and put in prison on the grounds of being a nuisance. Nothing more was heard of them; they simply disappeared. People began to be afraid, and they stopped reclaiming their lands and property for fear of meeting the same kind of fate. Threats and intimidations of various kinds were used against the monks and their teaching to diminish their influence and support amongst the people, and in this way the pillars of lamaism are being destroyed. Taxes were increased and compulsorily levied, thus crippling the monasteries' trade and income. This in time affected the monks' subsistence, and they were then forced to do secular work. Children are taken from the rightful ownership of parents. . . .'

The social benefits earlier introduced into Tibet supplied active centres of Chinese Communist propaganda. The primary schools, with a claimed enrolment of two thousand Tibetan students, taught more and more Chinese language, history and customs to the exclusion of things Tibetan. The five hundred Tibetan young men and women who had been selected and sent to study in the Central Nationality Academy were subjected to intensive Communist indoctrination and Tibetan dress, customs and aspirations were publicly ridiculed. Radio stations which had been set up in

Lhasa and Chamdo broadcast a steady stream of Chinese comment on current affairs, domestic and foreign. Film projector teams showed Chinese Communist documentaries throughout the country.

Even the Chinese papers more than hinted at the difficulties and privations the Tibetans were being made to suffer at the time. In an article in *Chung Kuo Fu Nu* (Chinese Women) the following picture was given:

'During the past several years patriotic women's associations or preparatory committees of patriotic women's associations were formed one after another in such big cities on the Tibetan plateau as Lhasa, Shigatse and Gyantse. Tibetan women of all levels are enthusiastically studying nationality policy, the constitution of the Chinese People's Republic, and the geography and history of the fatherland. . . . The broad masses of the Tibetan labouring women have positively participated in the various construction projects in Tibet. Thousands upon thousands of Tibetan women have joined in the construction of the Sikang-Tibet Highway, the Chinghai-Tibet Highway, the Lhasa-Shigatse Highway, and the Shigatse-Gyantse Highway, struggling stubbornly against lofty cliffs, torrential currents and muddy swamps. . . . Several thousands of Tibetan women from various villages and pastoral areas have organized themselves into auxiliary transportation teams, delivering on time millions of catties of provisions, materials and road-building tools to the constructions sites, along narrow winding paths. During the rainy season in the Pomi district along the Sikang-Tibet Highway the women took off their own dresses made of yak serge and used them to cover the grain they were sending to the road-builders. At night they slept in the caves or under the trees. . . .'

The greatest concentration of government activity, as distinct from military activity, was in Chamdo. In Lhasa there had been considerable reorganization of the various departments formerly used by the Lhasa Government, but no great pressure was imposed to hasten the innovations. Yet Chamdo was virgin as far as government administration was concerned and the Chinese went ahead with long-term plans to make it a chief centre of administration. They built an airfield which brought it within two hours' flying time of Chengtu, and the widened roads brought it within seven days' journey by truck from Chengtu, instead of the previous six weeks to two months. It was also an equally admirable centre for Sining and Lanchow to the north, and with the bulk of the Tibetan population living in East Tibet the Chinese could bring it more easily under the control of the Central Government in Peking.

After three years in Tibet it was still necessary for the Chinese to use Tibetans in these administrative posts, for following on the earlier Tibetan enthusiasm to join in the reconstructive and administrative activity, the growing Chinese oppression and Tibetan antipathy had increasingly isolated the Tibetans and made them more reluctant to have anything to do with the occupation forces. Thus an uneasy see-saw administrative arrangement obtained in which the Chinese would try to force through policies to the point of open defiance by the Tibetans, and the Tibetans would reject the policies they disliked just short of open rebellion.

The same situation was emerging in Lhasa to a lesser degree. After a great fanfare the Chinese announced the formation of a Lhasa branch of the People's Political Consultative Committee, with the Dalai Lama and Panchen Lama as members. However, when it was seen that everyone had to sit on chairs of equal height around the table the Tibetans objected to this levelling process being imposed on the Dalai Lama and refused to attend any more meetings until it was settled. When the Chinese announced that the Tibetan Army would be absorbed into the Chinese Army the Tibetans objected so sharply that the Chinese had to change their absorption plan to one of integration instead, letting the Tibetans keep their own units which were, however, to be trained by the Chinese.

Such unexpected intransigence on the part of the Tibetans, and the danger that their one extended supply route across Tibet might be destroyed by the rebellious Tibetans in East Tibet taking advantage of China's further military adventures into the border states, caused China to have second thoughts and temporarily stayed her hand.

The tempo of propaganda dropped, military preparations eased off, and a new policy of extensive social development was introduced throughout the country wherever the Chinese were in control.

CHAPTER 11

Tibetan Discontent Grows

On April 29, 1954, the 'Agreement between the People's Republic of China and the Republic of India on Trade and Communications between the Tibet region of China and India' was signed in Peking, according to a Chinese communiqué, 'bringing to an end the remnant privileges of the British and so establishing the relations between China and India, concerning Tibet, on a new basis'. The Agreement laid down five broad principles in addition to the liquidation of the Indian claims.

According to the Agreement India accepted the principle that Tibet constituted an integral part of China, and agreed to withdraw completely within six months the Indian contingent that had been stationed for decades at Yatung and Gyantse. Peking, it was stated, would render all assistance and facilities in aiding the withdrawal of Indian troops.

India agreed also to hand over all her property in Tibet to the Chinese authorities, leaving questions of detail regarding cost and manner of payment to be worked out later. These properties included all the telegraph, public telephone, and postal establishments, together with their equipment, and twelve rest houses situated in various parts of Tibet.

The Agreement, containing six articles, related only to the two issues of trade and pilgrim traffic. China would be permitted to open three trade agencies, in New Delhi, Calcutta and Kalimpong, while India would be allowed to establish similar offices at Yatung, Gyantse and Gartok. All trade and pilgrim traffic should henceforth be confined to six specific routes along the two thousand-mile common frontier.

The Trade Pact, as it was briefly called, was acclaimed in India and China and the five principles, outlined in the preamble, which formed the basis of the pact—mutual respect for each other's territorial integrity and sovereignty, mutual non-aggression, mutual non-interference in each other's internal affairs, equality and mutual benefit, and peaceful co-existence—became known as 'The Five Principles of Peaceful Co-Existence', or 'Panch Shila' in India, and were later taken up at Bandung as the accepted policy of the Afro-Asian bloc.

India gained practically nothing concrete from the pact. It was rumoured in Indian official circles that Mr. Nehru had hoped to obtain a fixed delineation of the hitherto vague border between Tibet and India, so limiting China's expansionist ambitions, but if this were the case it was another diplomatic defeat for India.

In a speech delivered in India's Lok Sabha on a debate on the international situation on May 15, 1954, Acharya T. B. Kripalani, the Leader of the Opposition, said:

'Recently we have entered into a treaty with China. This treaty concerns the whole of India. It does not concern a party or a person, it affects us all. We feel that China, after it had gone Communist, committed an act of aggression in Tibet. The plea is that China had the ancient right of suzerainty. This right was out of date, old and antiquated. It was theoretical; it was never exercised or very rarely exercised and even then in theory. It had lapsed by the flux of time. . . . I consider this as much a colonial aggression on the part of China as any colonial aggression indulged in by Western nations. The definition of colonialism is that one nation by force of arms and fraud occupies the territory of another nation. . . . Whether certain nations commit aggression against other peaceful nations does not always concern us. But in this case we are intimately concerned, because China has destroyed what is called a buffer state. In international politics, when a buffer state is destroyed by a powerful nation, that nation is considered to have committed aggression against its neighbours. . . . It is also well-known that in the new map of China other border territories like Nepal, Sikkim, etc., figure. This gives us an idea of the aggressive designs of China. . . . I do not say that because China conquered

Tibet we should have gone to war with it. It was possible. But we did well in not going to war. But this does not mean that we should recognize the claims of China in Tibet. We must know that it is an act of aggression against a foreign nation. It is as abominable as colonialism of any Western power. . . .'

While Prime Minister Nehru and Chou En-lai were being acclaimed throughout Asia for their magnanimous and enlightened approach to relations between nations, Tibet, which had been the object of discussion and agreement, took a radically different view. The growing bitterness against India felt by Tibetans of all classes since 1950, which they interpreted as cynical self-interest and betrayal, flared up into public demonstration inside Tibet.

Posters were printed and pasted on to walls throughout Lhasa, and copies were sent to all towns and monasteries in Tibet. The text was published in the *Tibet Mirror*, issued in Kalimpong on June 1, 1954:

'To Leaders, Officials, Monks, Soldiers, Traders, Craftsmen, Agriculturists, Nomads—the People of Tibet.

'This is to alert you to the great danger threatening our common cause, the independence of Tibet, regarding which I feel compelled to speak a few words.

'1. The last edition of the *Tibet Mirror* carried translations of articles from Indian papers of a trade pact signed at Peking between India and China regarding Tibet. There was a statement that "discussion in Peking related only to procedural matters and not to the substance of the issue". Neither was there any mention of which particular treaty formed the basis of the talks. Further, no full copy of the agreement was made public.

'2. Were the talks based on the Trade Regulations of 1893 or of 1908, both of which were mentioned in regard to the Peking Trade Agreement? If so, it is a violation of the Simla Convention of 1914 whereby both of those Trade Regulations are declared revoked in Clause 7.

'3. The Peking Trade Pact refers to Tibet as "an integral part of China", and there are many mentions of the "Tibet region of China", these being terms unprecedented in the history of Tibet and also another violation of the terms of the Simla Convention,

Clauses 3 and 9 of which first of all recognized the mutual independence of Tibet inasmuch as the Tibetan Government kept her existing rights, which until the time of the recent invasion of Tibet included the management of her external affairs; secondly, guaranteed the non-violation of Tibetan territory, Great Britain and China agreeing to abstain from sending their troops, stationing civil and military officers, or establishing colonies in Central Tibet.

'4. The Simla Convention was signed by the fully empowered representatives of the three Governments of Tibet, India and China, whereas the Peking Pact was concluded between India and China, *the wishes of the Government and people of Tibet being completely ignored.* This makes it clear that China wishes not only to absorb Tibet but to destroy our culture, religion and eventually our race by intermarriage, as is shown by their moves to try to get in, in addition to the two hundred and twenty thousand in the Liberation Army already in Tibet, a further two million Chinese for the so-called economic development of our country. It is only too obvious how our two neighbours are willing to come to private arrangements in favour of aggression so as to serve their own inter-Asian imperialist policies.

'5. Please read carefully the second Independent Treaty signed at Simla between Tibet and the British Government in India, on the same day, and immediately after, the Tripartite Simla Convention, as it recognized not the autonomy but the complete independence of Tibet, as follows:

' "The Government of China refusing to fix her official seal thereto and in default of which, all rights and privileges claimed by the Government of China in and with regard to Tibet, are hereby declared revoked." '

The protest, circulating in Tibetan inside a closed Tibet, evoked no sympathy or response either in India or the outside world.

What was extremely significant about its widespread circulation inside Tibet was the fact that the anti-Chinese demands were now so numerous and strongly entrenched that such could now be printed and distributed throughout the country without detection of the organizers.

The chief anti-Chinese organization involved in the demonstrations and pamphleteering was a group known as the *Mi-mang Tsong-du* (or People's Party). While nationalist and subversive, they limited themselves to public demonstrations against unpopular Chinese Communist measures and took no part in violent activities of any form. Notices appeared on the walls of buildings overnight denouncing or mocking the Chinese occupation personnel; Chinese notices were torn down or besmeared with manure; Chinese parades or demonstrations were bombarded from densely packed crowds with dried yak dung and stones, or there were cleverly organized 'silences'. When the Chinese arrested some of the more prominent and handed them over for trial to the Tibetan courts they were released shortly afterwards on 'insufficient evidence', or some other bland reason. At their own demonstrations they could number four or five thousand people, and the Chinese dared do no more than arrest some of the more extreme orators and even then, as indicated, only hand them over to the Tibetan courts with complaints.

In June 1954 the Dalai Lama received an invitation from the Chinese Government to visit Peking and other places in China. The invitation evoked an immediate protest in Tibet and there were many demonstrations to protest against the Dalai Lama leaving the country, the general suspicion being that he would not be permitted to return.

In addition to demonstrations the *Mi-mang Tsong-du* in Lhasa secretly organized a mass revolt on the day scheduled for the Dalai Lama's departure, when thousands of Tibetans were to throw themselves in the Dalai Lama's path so that he could not pass through them without having to walk over their bodies. The Chinese got word of their plans, and several days before the scheduled date of departure moved the Dalai Lama to a relative's house and from there on his way to China.

However, the Chinese were unpleasantly surprised by the intensity of the feeling shown by the Tibetans to their invitation to the Dalai Lama and gave strong assurances that he would be well treated in China. On the other hand, it did not prevent them from engineering at least two attempts on the Dalai Lama's life on his way to China. On one occasion a bridge mysteriously collapsed just after the Dalai Lama had crossed over, and the Chinese blamed Kham bandits; and on another occasion a landslide almost carried the party away.

The Panchen Lama had also been invited to visit China at the same time. For some while the Chinese had been building up the Panchen Lama's influence in Tibet, both to undermine the Dalai Lama's prestige and to seek to divide the Tibetans into two camps over the centuries-old controversy so that they could be dealt with more easily.

After Britain, China and Tibet had signed the Tripartite Treaty in 1914 the then Panchen Lama, who was very pro-Chinese, was forced to flee in 1920 to China where the Kuomingtang Party was emerging as the new government. Right away the Panchen Lama began scheming with the Kuomingtang officials to support him with money, arms and men to re-enter Tibet, but the new Kuomingtang Government was in no position to indulge in such adventures.

In 1933 the Thirteenth Dalai Lama died. During his reign it had been virtually impossible for a Chinese national, civil or military, to enter Tibet, but as it usually took several months or years to discover a reincarnation of the Dalai Lama the ageing Panchen Lama prevailed upon the Kuomingtang Government to assist him in 'liberating' Tibet. On this occasion help was given, and while the Chinese forces were converging on Tibet's eastern borders a Chinese goodwill mission was sent to Lhasa to persuade a leaderless Tibetan Government to accept a permanent Chinese delegation in Lhasa on grounds of common cultural and religious ties. As a direct result of this offensive, in 1935 a meeting was called in Lhasa and it was decided that the Panchen Lama should be allowed to re-enter Tibet accompanied by his household and a few followers, but before he could take advantage of this the Panchen Lama died in China.

When the new reincarnation of the Dalai Lama was discovered in 1938 in Amdo Province a new reincarnation of the Panchen Lama was found in that same year and in the same province. The position of this reincarnation, however, was still unsettled as there was a simultaneous discovery of two other claimants in Lhasa. According to custom the authorities in Lhasa requested the Amdo claimant to appear in Lhasa for verification of his claims, but the Chinese authorities, for obvious reasons of their own, refused to comply with this request and some years later, without consultation with Lhasa, officially installed their protégé as the new Panchen Lama. When the Kuomingtang Government was defeated and fled to Formosa the Chinese Communist Government took over the care and training of the Amdo Panchen Lama.

In 1950, 'at the request of the Panchen Lama', the Chinese ordered the People's Liberation Army into Tibet, and in 1951 the Panchen Lama was present for the talks conducted by the Chinese Communists with the Tibetan goodwill mission on the special initiative of the Peking Government. The pact which recognized China's suzerainty over Tibet acknowledged also the Amdo reincarnation as the true Panchen Lama. In 1952 the newly declared Panchen Lama, escorted by a strong force of Chinese troops, entered Lhasa, and from that time the Chinese had made every effort to build him up politically, but the Tibetan Government and people, while accepting the installation under force of circumstances, refused to recognize him as anything more than a spiritual figure. The Chinese tried by every means to override the objections of the Tibetan people and on every public occasion introduced the Panchen Lama as an equal to the Dalai Lama.

After being in China several months the Dalai Lama and Panchen Lama were invited to attend a meeting of the Chinese State Council on March 9, 1955, where they were forced to submit to a number of decisions on Tibetan affairs. One of these decisions was the establishment of a 'Preparatory Committee for the Autonomous Region of Tibet'. The Committee consisted of fifty-one members, fifteen from the Lhasa administration, ten from the 'Panchen Lama's Bureau', ten from the Chamdo 'People's Liberation Committee', eleven from monasteries and 'People's Organizations', and five representing the Chinese Government, with the Dalai Lama being named a chairman. It was announced that the members of the Committee were appointed 'with the approval of the Chinese State Council' and the three regions of Tibet were subordinate to it. It was also stated that the chief task of the Preparatory Committee was to prepare for regional automony in accordance with the provisions of the Chinese Constitution, the Agreement of 1951 and the concrete circumstances of Tibet. The first meeting of this Preparatory Committee was held on April 22, 1956, and thereafter there were in the next three years twenty-seven meetings out of which the Dalai Lama was present at and presided over twenty-five. But on his arrival in India the Dalai Lama stated at Tezpur on April 15, 1959, that 'in practice, even this body had little power and decisions in all important matters were taken by the Chinese authorities'.

In China during the visit of the two Lamas the Peking Government went out of its way to show preference for the Panchen Lama on every occasion, presumably to impress upon the Dalai Lama how they were prepared to treat those who co-operated with them. If this were so the rather naïve policy had exactly the opposite effect, and as the Dalai Lama went about the country, saying the proper things prepared for him by his hosts but noting particularly their attitude towards religion, the complete absorption in ruthless materialistic policies, the cynical playing off of the Panchen Lama against himself to further their own ends, he came to certain very definite conclusions in his own mind. He said nothing to anyone at the time, not even to Mr. Nehru, whom he met in Peking during the Indian Prime Minister's visit to China, and who asked him in a private conversation if there was anything India could do to help Tibet, and it was only later that I was able to find out his impressions from his family.

Meanwhile in Tibet the Tibetans were becoming uneasy at the unduly prolonged visit which seemed to confirm their suspicions that the Chinese were going to hold the Dalai Lama in China as a hostage. Demonstrations were organized in Lhasa by the Mi-mang Tsong-du demanding his early return, and even in Kalimpong there was a mass protest and public prayers. From Tingri in West Tibet, an area noted for its fighters, several hundred Tibetans marched to Lhasa to add their voices to the general request and also threaten armed action if the Dalai Lama were not returned immediately.

If the Chinese had ideas about the Dalai Lama they were quickly changed in view of this ominous reaction and he was permitted to return to Tibet.

Shortly after his arrival in Lhasa evidence of his new attitude to Communist China began to appear, both directly and indirectly. Immediately there was a hardening of official opposition to Chinese proposals. The move by the Chinese to have Chinese paper currency substituted for the silver Tibetan currency was flatly rejected, and the offer of economic integration with China refused. The Chinese then countered with an order that only traders with letters of credit issued by the Bank of China and negotiable in branches in India would be allowed to trade—and found themselves with a monumental leakage of Chinese silver coins being smuggled into India. They failed to elicit any enthusiasm for their project and the Preparatory Committee for the Autonomous Region of Tibet became increasingly exasperated by Tibetan excuses at inability to attend.

On the 23rd day of the Tibetan fifth month (July-August) 1955 the Dalai Lama made a public speech in Norbulinka, the summer palace. After reviewing the history of Tibet and pointing out that when there was a balanced emphasis on both religion and politics the country had prospered, but that when politics took prominence over religion to the exclusion of the latter there was national deterioration, he went on:

'At present and in the future we shall carry out many new changes both in our religious and political life, and this is the urgent task which faces us. But in what way can we make progress? Today our Tibetan people are facing many difficulties from every side. We have no strength of our own and we have no political experience. We have no means to progress in any way. It is for this reason that the Chinese Communists have sent their men here to help us in the reconstruction of Tibet. But we must recognize very clearly that the Chinese Communists have not come here to control us, or become our masters, or to oppress us. We should adopt a friendly attitude towards them.

'If the Chinese Communists have come to Tibet to help us, it is most important that they should respect the Tibetan people's own social system, culture, customs and habits, and honour the wishes of the whole people of Tibet, and not obstruct or do damage to the high principles of our nation. If the Chinese Communist personnel in Tibet do not understand the conditions, and harm or injure our people, you should immediately report the facts to the Government. The Government will certainly take steps to make them correct their ways. If the Chinese Communists do not correct their ways our Government can immediately ask for their expulsion.

'I hope all our Tibetan people will take upon themselves the responsibility for carrying out the various tasks allotted to them. For example, if the members of a family can themselves control and carry out the affairs of the family that family may be said to be a self-managed family or an independent one. A country is also in the same position as a family. I sincerely hope that the officials of the Government and the people will stand at their posts, will remain determined in their attitudes, carrying out their responsibilities and using their full strength in performing their duties.

'Today I am very pleased with the officials of the Government and the people and thank them for working extremely hard for the welfare of their district, Government and country. But there are some officials and people who have a very narrow outlook and cannot take a broad view of things. For their own selfish advancement and under the attraction of glittering gold they do not care for the good of the country and the people, they practise oppression and deceit, they give trouble to the people and harm the Government, and thus are responsible for great harm to the country. I would request such people to correct their former mistakes and, becoming new men, atone for their misdeeds in the interests of the country and the people. Besides them there are some few people who disregard their national culture and history, consider themselves to be progressive, and who have changed their ways to doing what they like in a very confused manner. I regard such ideas as mistaken. Progress cannot be attained suddenly in a confused manner and must be attained gradually in an ordered way. Again, there are Government officials who are envious of each other, create conflicts and bitterness, and cannot cooperate with each other. Because they fritter away their energies they cannot carry out the work of the administration effectively. I desire that they give up their selfish attitude and take a broad view of things, correct each other and become united together. Only by doing so can we create and develop our strength. For example, it is not possible for a single person to lift a big stone using his own strength, but if the strength of several people is pooled together it becomes very easy to lift the same stone. This is a very simple example but I know that all of you will pay special attention to this matter.

'Tibet consists of Kham, Tsang, Ü and Amdo, and all consist of the Tibetan people. Their spirit and way of living all have such intimate connexions that they cannot be separated from each other. I hope that all of you will deeply think over this matter, love each other, and be united with each other, and not become separated from each other.

'Finally, I hope that the people of the whole of Tibet by their unity and co-operation will increase our strength and put all their energies into the construction of a new Tibet based on the unity of political life and religion.'

This outspoken speech was wildly acclaimed in Lhasa and other parts of Tibet for it marked the emergence of the Dalai Lama on the political scene in favour of a united 'Greater Tibet' without Chinese occupation, and it immediately encouraged and strengthened the hands of the anti-Chinese groups throughout the country.

Two months later the Mi-mang Tsong-du came out publicly with an even stronger declaration.

'We Tibetan people make the following appeal because we oppose the Chinese Communists who are destroying all our customs and systems, and also because of the complete breach of the Seventeen-Point Sino-Tibetan Agreement signed by them. . . .

'But speaking about the present situation in Tibet we declare that our religion is facing a very grave crisis which has thrown us into the very deep valley of darkness and destruction. The Dalai

9. Chagpuri, or 'Hospital Hill', a garrison occupied by the Tibetan army at the time of the revolt in March, 1959, which was heavily shelled and destroyed by the Chinese Communists

10. Kangting, or Tachienlu, strategic border town in Kham

11. The Potala, the Dalai Lama's winter palace, the walls of which were damaged by shelling during the revolt

Lama has been robbed of his political and religious powers. The future of the Tibetan nation is facing as grave a danger as a candle-light in a severe storm. The root cause of this crisis is the oppressive ways in which the Chinese Communists have been forcing Communist ideas upon the Tibetan people, the most deplorable policy of violence practised by the Chinese Communists, and the failure of the Chinese Communists to implement any of the promises made by them to the Tibetan people. In order to save our country from this dangerous future we have already, on a previous occasion, made a formal protest to the Chinese Government and the Dalai Lama.

'Formerly, under the Dalai Lama, there were Regents, Kashag and the various other Government organizations which carried out the administration of the whole of Tibet. But since the occupation of Tibet by the Chinese Communists all the former organizations of the Government have ceased to function and the Chinese Communists have established a large number of illegal organizations in their place to carry out the administration. . . . The Chinese Communists have not only increased administrative organizations but they have also established organizations such as the "Patriotic Youth League" and the "Chinese Schools", with the sole object of forcibly indoctrinating the youth of Tibet in Communism, and thus to destroy the culture and civilization of the nation. Moreover, in opposition to the will of the people the Chinese Communists have destroyed the social system of Tibet in which political and religious life are joined together, and have also destroyed the religion of the Tibetan people. Therefore we, in the name of the people of Tibet, have come forward to appeal to the Dalai Lama. We request that the Dalai Lama stop the organization of the "Patriotic Youth League", close the "Chinese Schools" and prevent the indoctrination of the Tibetan people in Communism by the Chinese Communists. We are now resolved not to accept the establishment of the proposed Regional Autonomous Government in Tibet as we already have the Government of the Dalai Lama. At the same time we also request the Chinese Communist Military Representative in Tibet to allow us to go to Peking to lodge this protest. If the Chinese Communists disregard the people's wishes, and by force, oppression and violence suppress the earnest appeal of the people, we, in the name of all the people of Tibet, are fully resolved to shed our blood and sacrifice our lives to oppose the Communists and we shall definitely not co-operate in any of the activities of the Chinese Communists in Tibet.'

CHAPTER 12

India Learns of Impending Revolt

With the deterioration of the Chinese position in Tibet, except militarily, the Indian Government decided to try to secure some advantage from the situation. Indian prestige amongst Tibetans, both inside and outside Tibet, could not be lower, for the Tibetans held that India was afraid of China, was inept in her diplomacy, and callous in her cynical disregard of what happened in Tibet.

In the autumn of 1954 I was asked by an Indian Government official to advise on what might be done to redeem India's prestige in some way. The matter would have to be carefully handled, for with the international acclaim following on the signing of the Sino-Indian Trade Pact and the subsequent success of the 'Five Principles of Peaceful Co-existence' at Bandung, India must not be caught out in any subversive action concerning the affairs of Tibet. I was not at all sanguine that anything could be done with the material available in Kalimpong, and I said so. Although many Tibetans had returned to Tibet after the Chinese take-over in 1951, others had elected to stay in Kalimpong. Amongst them were several former high officials in the Lhasa Government, and they had bought houses and land and settled down for a long stay in India. Having nothing else to do with their time they indulged in their favourite pastime of inter-family feudal politics.

There were several major cliques, and a host of other minor factions, in the intrigues which went on constantly in the town and, through messengers, in Tibet. There was the major division of the pro-Panchen Lama group, who had been given new life and authority by the support of the Chinese Government, from the followers of the Dalai Lama. Then there was the group formed by the Tibetan members of the Sikkim and Bhutan royal families and their relatives inside Tibet—a powerful faction, for some of the leading acting and former ministers of Tibet were related to them. There was the Shakabpa group which had inherited its influence from Shakabpa's association with the former Regent, Takta Rimpoche, and his leadership of the various delegations just before the Chinese communist occupation of Tibet. There was the Gyalu Thondup group which looked to him, as an older brother of the Dalai Lama, for leadership. And there were the Tibetan Association, the Indo-Tibet Association, the various Khamba family loyalty groups—Pangdatshang, Sadutshang and others. Each was suspicious of the other's motives and jealous lest any one of them should be successful in some contact with an outside power or acquire some influence which would give them precedence over the other.

The Shakabpa group was suspect because Shakabpa stood for a return to the *status quo* in Tibet, and many of the Tibetans were determined that once the Chinese were got rid of the old régime, too, must be changed. The Sikkim-Bhutan family lacked support because, rightly or wrongly, they were suspected of desiring power only for financial and prestige reasons. The Gyalu Thondup group was distrusted by the others because Gyalu Thondup had been away in China for a long period, broken only by a visit of a few months to Tibet in 1952; further, although he had the advantage of being a member of the Dalai Lama's family, he lacked initiative and was inclined to submit to the political pressures from Communist China or India. The minor factions functioned on a lower and more local level of intrigue.

With such an evident lack of cohesion and unity I knew that any thought of successful, or even useful, activity was out of the question. Even if all the groups could in some way be got together they could still do nothing to overthrow the Chinese rule in Tibet. They represented leading families, estates and official positions, but had little actual strength in terms of manpower. Even with the Tibetan Army behind them—and that required a monumental effort of the imagination—they still presented a negligible obstacle to the Chinese.

The only possible hope that Tibet had of getting rid of the Chinese lay with the Kham and Amdo Tibetans of East Tibet. Not only were they the most populous in the whole country, but their fearless fighting qualities, their knowledge of mountain warfare and their implacable hatred of the Chinese added up to an opposition that might prove insuperable to the Chinese. The difficulty, of course, of harnessing them to the cause of Tibetan unity lay in their violent antipathy to the officials of the Lhasa Government.

I knew how they felt about the Lhasa Government, but I also knew that they were loyal Tibetans and loyal to the Dalai Lama. All that was required to bridge the gap was someone who could speak for Kham and yet be prepared, for the sake of Tibet, to work with the very weak and disparate elements of Lhasa officialdom. Only one person filled this requirement, Rapga Pangdatshang, and he was in Kham and was forbidden by law to enter India.

I told the Government official all this. The only possibility of doing anything lay with Rapga Pangdatshang. If the Indians would rescind their expulsion order, I said, I was certain that Rapga would leave Kham, come to India and work for Tibetan independence from China, bringing in Topgyay, his brother, and the other leaders in Amdo, with their followers.

After consultation with New Delhi my plan was adopted. I sent a note to Rapga, in a bottle of medicine which I knew he would open and use, informing him that if he wanted to come to India now the way was open. In March 1955 Rapga Pangdatshang arrived in India, his appearance in Kalimpong renewing speculation there, as no one knew that I had sent for him. Was he an envoy of the Chinese come to spy on the Tibetan officials in Kalimpong? Was he a tool of the Chinese, sent to Kalimpong to bring over the other Tibetans to the Communists, or was he part of the Chinese take-over plans for the border areas? No one could believe that he had resigned his influential position in the East Tibetan Autonomous Government just to come to India to see his son and settle some business affairs.

The scholarly, inscrutable Rapga paid little attention to the many rumours circulating about him. To me, accepted as a member of the Pangdatshang family because of my long association with them in Kham, he was completely frank, and to the Indian officials who approached him about doing something in Tibet he was disturbingly so.

It appeared that after serving on the Chamdo Liberation Committee and as Governor of Markham in East Tibet in 1953 he resigned from his political activities on grounds of ill health and retired to one of the Pangdatshang estates to write a book on the history of Tibet. After almost two years of this he thought he could safely make all arrangements for a visit to Lhasa without arousing the suspicions of the Chinese. However, as it happened the Chinese were anxious that he should act as one of the Kham representatives to the newly-constituted fifty-one member Preparatory Committee for the Autonomous Region of Tibet. Quite apart from the trouble the Chinese were experiencing in having it accepted by the Lhasa officials, the Kham and Amdo Tibetans were very angry that they should only have been allocated eight members out of the fifty-one—five of which were Chinese. The Chinese were hopeful that Rapga would use his influence to persuade the Khambas to accept their proposals and they agreed, albeit reluctantly, to his request that he should visit Lhasa and India for a few months to settle his affairs first. He had been making arrangements for this trip when he had received my letter.

If the Indian officials had hoped for a quiet, scholarly organizer of anti-Communist propaganda they were shatteringly disappointed. Rapga refused point-blank to collect information, or list numbers of Chinese soldiers in different places, or write articles and pamphlets for clandestine distribution. These were tasks that could be done by any lesser fry who might be interested. He was only interested in complete revolution, overthrow of the Chinese Communists, reform of the Tibetan Government, and the recognition of the new Popular Government by the other nations of the world. He had made the journey to India with this in view and would accept nothing less. If the Indian and other governments were not prepared to help or co-operate in any way then, of course, the Tibetans would be disappointed but it would in no way affect their determination to revolt, and the outside countries would just have to adjust their policies accordingly. The anti-Chinese feeling in East Tibet was now so great that the Kham and Amdo leaders would either have to lead their people in the fighting against the Chinese or be killed by them as collaborators. No amount of talking or writing could stop the inevitable uprising, and it was because of this that he had made the trip to Lhasa to co-ordinate the Kham-Amdo Tibetans with the anti-Chinese Mi-mang Tsong-du in Lhasa in a nation-wide uprising.

While in Lhasa he had got into touch with one of the leaders of the Mi-mang Tsong-du, a revolutionary friend of former years, but the contact had to be by writing as he was being closely watched by the Chinese. He informed him that there were about a hundred thousand Tibetans in East Tibet ready to fight and he asked how many might be expected in Lhasa. His friend replied that the Lhasa anti-Chinese groups were not yet ready to join in any armed uprising and he, Rapga, doubted if they ever would.

His information rocked the Indian Government, who had only hoped to salvage some prestige from the earlier diplomatic débâcles by working quietly to counteract the steady flow of Chinese Communist propaganda against India. A Tibet in revolt, denouncing China as an aggressor, would seriously embarrass India, now the Afro-Asian champion of the 'Five Principles of Peaceful Co-existence' signed over the presumed national corpse of Tibet. The ruthless suppression of an Asian nation by another Asian nation, China, while a third Asian nation, India, both connived with it and advocated a policy of non-aggression and non-interference, was something that would destroy the prestige of both nations not only in Asia but throughout the world.

When their attempts to persuade Rapga to modify the Kham-Amdo aims failed the Indian officials changed their tactics. They pointed out how hopeless the Tibetan position was, impressing upon him how inadequately armed the Tibetans were with their obsolete weapons against a nation which had just withstood the armies of the United Nations in Korea. Rapga in turn observed that he and the Tibetans involved were more likely to know what arms they had, and what their chances of success against the

Chinese were, as they had been living with the Chinese occupation forces and their lives were forfeit. He gave it as their opinion that they could inflict such losses on the Chinese in three months as to make them anxious to negotiate. This would not be due to military pressure alone, but also to the fact that the Chinese would not wish to make an international issue out of Tibet. He and the others were prepared to gamble their lives on the outcome but they wanted recognition by the outside Powers of the Tibetan revolt and claims for independence, and their help in forcing reforms on the Lhasa Government to make it more representative of the people.

When word of the new situation in Tibet reached the U.S. authorities they were immediately interested. After preliminary discussions with officials in India an official from Washington, in the guise of a tourist, was flown to India for secret personal talks with Rapga. I acted as interpreter and we met on several occasions for discussions over a period of four days. He informed Rapga that he understood that there was a movement for self-determination in Tibet and that Rapga had proposals for accomplishing this which necessitated help from America. He was there to find out what help was required and how that help could be given. Was the help to be local or national? Was it to be for Kham only, or was it to include the whole of 'Greater Tibet'? Was it to be political, diplomatic, economic, or military?

When Rapga had outlined the situation as he had done to the Indian officials the American official expressed sympathy with Tibet in its predicament but pointed out the difficulties involved in sending supplies of military equipment or personnel to Tibet, particularly in view of its contiguity with non-violent, neutralist, anti-American India. Rapga agreed with him and expressed his own doubt that India would do anything with her present policy and attitude *vis-à-vis* Tibet and China. It was because of this that he felt it absolutely essential that Tibet should revolt and present India and other countries with a *fait accompli*.

The American official stressed that co-operation with the Indian Government was essential, and that Tibet's future friendly relations with India depended upon this. He also pointed out its importance from the point of view that in the event of Tibet making any claim to independence before the United Nations it was imperative that she have the support of India and, through India, that of Afro-Asia and the Middle East. Recognition by the U.S. and other western powers would be almost automatic, but if the West took the lead in such recognition it would immediately antagonize the Communist bloc and thus jeopardize Tibet's chances. Given these considerations the American official then went on to draw up with Rapga a programme of assistance for Tibet which he would suggest to the U.S. authorities on his return.

Briefly, the programme would cover a ten-year period in which Tibet would receive help, as that was the minimum time required for revolution against an occupying power, the overthrow of feudal-collaborationist government and the establishment of a new government and state of sufficient stability and authority to be recognized by the U.N. The American official then assumed, for the sake of planning, an initial period of five years in which the preliminary stages of revolution, overthrow of reactionary government and establishing of tutelage government would occur, for which representatives from districts all over Tibet, including instructed clergy, should be assembled in a Political Consultative Committee.

Keeping in mind that a combination of factors might precipitate the revolution at any time, perhaps in the next few months, it was agreed that Rapga should aim in the first year at organization. This was to include the primary organization of a national entity, and the resolution of inter-provincial disputes, the inter-family jealousies and feuds, and the inter-religious divisions (Dalai Lama versus Panchen Lama). The purpose of this period of organization would not just be 'anti-Communist' in emphasis, or simply to draw a line of demarcation which would seem to indicate who, among the officials and leaders, should be considered for the new Government, but to propagate simple instructions through slogans on such subjects as land reform, reform of compulsory labour, deportations, forced trade, and all forms of enforced tax imposed by the old feudal and now Communist régimes; to prepare for government participation and administration; and to put forward other such principles which could be easily grasped by the people of Tibet to associate them in loyalty to the new Government in its proposed reforms.

All this would have to be planned and initiated so that there would be no hiatus in the transition period from the old Government to the new, and so that the Tibetans could ultimately conduct all administration themselves without the help of other countries.

They also discussed the economic possibilities of Tibet, its mineral resources, the chances of oil and uranium being found, and in a more immediate context the possibility of taking up, in the talks then being held between the U.S. and China at Geneva, the question of Tibet's export of wool.

The foregoing programme was only a very tentative outline of proposals which the American official said he would put before the appropriate officials on his return to the U.S. He would also suggest that a special American agent be appointed who would have no contact with the U.S. Embassy but who, he gave Rapga to understand, would be officially assigned to handle Tibetan affairs. In the meantime Rapga could go ahead doing what he could in the matter of organizing and giving assurance and hope of support to loyal anti-Chinese Communist elements inside Tibet.

Part Three

REVOLT

CHAPTER 13

Revolt in Kham and Amdo

In February 1956 major revolts broke out in several places in
East Tibet which were so distant from each other that it was
obvious some measure of co-ordination in plans had taken place.

The Chinese Government later claimed that the link between
Lhasa and the Kham leaders was first made as early as 1954–5
when the Dalai Lama visited China. They stated that the Kashag
appointed some officials in the Dalai Lama's entourage—Surkong
Wongching-Galie, a cabinet minister, and another junior official,
Shudrun Lobsang Yeshi (my friend of 1950 days in Kalimpong)—
to discuss plans for revolt with the Kham leaders when they
travelled through East Tibet on their journeys to and from China.
It is difficult at this stage to find out if this is true, but certainly
Shudrun Lobsang Yeshi was one of the key figures in the Lhasa
revolt and died in the fighting there.

A few months previously Lobsang Tsewong, the Amdo Tibetan
leader and Vice-President of Tsinghai under the Chinese, had been
arrested for speaking out against the iniquities of the Chinese
Communist land reform in Tibet and had been taken down-
country to somewhere in China. This precipitated a series of local
uprisings and demonstrations against the Chinese in Amdo, and
the Peking Government ordered more troops into the area to
disarm once for all the rebellious Tibetan tribesmen. When one
unit of two hundred arrived in the Golok area the Golok tribesmen captured them, disarmed them, cut off their noses, and sent
them back to their garrisons thus mutilated as a warning of what
was likely to happen to other Chinese. The Chinese then sent
several thousand troops into the mountains and the Goloks, with

the help of an Amdo Tibetan, Dorji Pasang, chieftain of over a hundred thousand families in Dzachuka and leader of rebels since 1952, killed between seven and eight thousand before the Chinese were forced to retreat.

In the Derge area a nomad chieftain, Chagun Thupden, and a member of the great Kham trading family of Sadutshang, Lonyendra, led two successful groups of rebels against Chinese troops stationed there.

In the garrison town of Litang, over fourteen thousand feet in the mountains, the Chinese had tried to head off the revolt by attempting to disarm the inhabitants of the town and large monastery, but they were defeated and the large arsenal and treasury looted by the now rampant Tibetans.

Batang, which had been one of the first towns in Kham to turn Communist in 1950, and which had provided the Chinese with more Tibetan quislings than any other town in Tibet, also erupted into revolt. In a single attack the Tibetans there captured every garrison and official building in a matter of hours, killing over a thousand Chinese. Unfortunately they were too late in capturing the post and telegraph offices and a Chinese official radioed the news of the revolt down-country before he was killed.

The leader of the revolt in Batang wrote me a letter in which, after recording Chinese atrocities in Kham, he said:

'According to the Communists, if the Tibetans were not satisfied to abide by the teachings of Mao Tse-tung there were three possibilities open to them: they could turn to America for help, or to the Nationalist Government of Chiang Kai-shek, or they could commit suicide. It was a dangerous policy to pursue, for it meant that divisive and rebellious elements increased not only amongst the Tibetans but also amongst Mao's own forces. But whether we live or die we are not fools to be deceived by slippery tongues. We would rather fight to the death as becomes our spirit than be forced into slow extinction as cowards. . . .

'From time to time our people rebelled against the charges of the Communists, and the measures enforced against them. Nor were the vicissitudes that we were called upon to pass through during this period due to any treaties or secret agreements made with foreign agents, or any other act of treachery. If there is any explanation of our sufferings it must lie in the doctrine of Karma, that we are reaping the fruit of our past misdeeds, and we would not deny the universality of this principle. . . .

'Spontaneous uprisings broke out all over the country, with revenge as the prime motive in almost every instance. It was known to be a hopeless fight but we could no longer contain ourselves. In one place aeroplanes bombarded us for five days in three waves of bombers a day. Everywhere there were scenes of slaughter and promiscuous butchery. What could small, ill-equipped groups of Tibetans do against innumerable Chinese soldiers equipped with everything? Monasteries, towns, heaps of human corpses and ruined fields presented a picture of chaos and bleak gloom. There was no end to the Chinese offensive. On the sixth day pamphlets were dropped urging the people to repent of the wrongs committed. . . .

'Without warning the Chinese bombed the monastery of Ba-Chyo-De, the chief seat of the Tsong-ka-pa sect, fifteen times until it was levelled to the ground. Some of the rarest books of the Gelugba doctrine vanished in the bombardment. Not content with this, the soldiers followed it up by burning the remnants. Tashi Naljor, who was conspicuous by his bravery in the fighting, was beaten to death along with others. A gigantic statue of Gewa Jampo, Maitrya Buddha, measuring three storeys high, was desecrated and smashed to pieces by axes. Sacred prayer leaves enclosed within the statue were thrown into the river. . . .

'Litang also met with the same ruthless fate. A colossal statue of Sakyamuni Buddha, built under the patronage of Sonam Gyaltso, Dalai Lama of Tibet, was smashed and destroyed. The itinerant professor of Litang monastery, Lobsang Kechun, aged about eighty, died. Thousands were thrown into prison. In the nearby monastery of Ju-dechen-ling only fifteen out of three hundred monks escaped death. . . .

'The Dzong-bon (local Governor) was the most unfortunate of all. Ropes were tied around his neck and he was led through the market-place. There he was fastened to a pillar and subjected to a slow-torture death. Cold and hot water alternately, according to the time of day, was trickled on to his head. Friends and acquaintances were forced to slap him, to spit in his face, while the Chinese jeered at him. . . .

'Almost the whole of the population of Kham was reduced to slavery, and a terrible time of oppression followed. The Khambas who were captured were forced to dig their own graves, and were shot beside the graves they had dug. On many occasions young girls were forced to stab the helpless prisoners to death. Many were buried alive.'

Little of this filtered through to the outside world. The London *Times* correspondent sent a despatch from Nepal that some fighting had been reported in East Tibet and a few hundred Chinese were presumed killed. A few other papers carried an inside half-column or some other vague rumours picked up in Kalimpong, but apart from these the matter was passed over.

In Kalimpong itself Rapga Pangdatshang was disillusioned. No further word had been received from the Americans. He had approached Shakabpa, as the leading Tibetan official of the Lhasa Government in Kalimpong, about doing something to help, but Shakabpa had claimed that he had given up all politics and was only residing in Kalimpong as an ordinary citizen. Strangely enough, only a week after Rapga's conversation with him and after Rapga had outlined the Kham and Amdo Tibetans' plans for the revolt for Tibetan independence, Rapga had a visit from an Indian official to warn him against participating in any politics while in India and telling him the gist of what he had secretly passed on to Shakabpa. This, plus the lukewarm reaction of some other Tibetan officials to his proposals, conclusively destroyed any hopes Rapga had still nurtured that a more enlightened outlook might now exist amongst those who had held official positions in the former Lhasa Government. From now on he was determined to have nothing to do with them, and to direct his activities to installing a government composed of Tibetans from Kham and Amdo.

In Lhasa the Chinese moved swiftly to counteract the effects of the revolt in East Tibet. The Peking *Jan Min Jih Pao* of April 25, 1956, carried the full text of the Dalai Lama's report at the in-

augural meeting of the Preparatory Committee for the Autonomous Region of Tibet. Following, are excerpts:

'Vice-Premier Chen (Chen Yi) and members of the Central
Government Delegation, members of the Preparatory Committee,
and various delegates: under the wise and correct leadership and
concern of the Chinese Communist Party and the Central People's
Government, and of Chairman Mao, who is the great and respected
leader of the people of all nationalities of our country, the Preparatory Committee for the Autonomous Regions of Tibet is now
officially inaugurated. This is another brilliant achievement of the
Chinese Communist Party's nationality policy. It not only shows
greater unity within Tibet but also unites the increasing consolidation and growth of unity and co-operation among the peoples of
all nationalities in the country. . . .' (In this passage the word
nationalities means the five nationalities which, in the Chinese
view, make up the Chinese people.—Author.)

'All the successive ruling classes in the past adopted an oppressive policy against the people of Tibet, as well as against other
nationalities in the country. Particularly so did the Manchu
Dynasty and the KMT reactionary Government, who cruelly
oppressed and exploited the people of various minorities but who
yielded timidly to imperialist aggression. Thus the Tibetan
people's historical suspicions and fears were greatly aggravated,
and there were even originated the ideas and behaviour of trying
to become separated from the big family of the mother country.
As a result the relations between Tibet and the motherland became
more and more estranged.

'Since then the political, economic and cultural undertakings of
Tibet for a long time remained backward and stagnant. The
people's living condition changed from bad to worse. On the
other hand, the imperialists utilized the hostile feelings of the
Tibetan people against the Manchu Court and the KMT revolutionary Government, and carried out all kinds of inducement and
instigation in the attempt to make the Tibetan people turn against
the motherland and place themselves under imperialist oppression
and enslavement. Particularly, at the moment when the entire
mainland was about to be completely liberated, the oppressors

madly redoubled their rumour-mongering activities to slander the Communist Party, tempting the Tibetan people to obstruct liberation. . . .

'Since the founding of the People's Republic of China and the Central People's Government was officially proclaimed in 1949, the Central People's Government, in accordance with the provisions of the Common Programme of the Chinese People's Political Conference, completely abolished the oppressive policy towards the nationalities, announced that all nationalities are equal within the territory of the People's Republic of China, enforced the principle of unity and mutual assistance, opposed imperialism and the people's enemies within the various nationalities, and turned the People's Republic of China into a large family of friendship and co-operation of all nationalities. . . .

'During the past five years the People's Liberation Army units and the working personnel that came to Tibet have consciously followed and executed the nationality policy laid down by the Chinese Communist Party and Chairman Mao. They deal with the people of Tibetan nationality with brotherly affection, listen to their opinions, give consideration to their interests in all spheres, and fully consult the local Tibetan leaders in all matters. . . .'

There was more of this, all in the same line, and obviously prepared by a Party propagandist. Most, if not all of it was for outside consumption, of course, either through the Indian Consulate to the outside world or through the normal channels of the China News Agency in Peking and Hong Kong. It was certainly not for the people of Lhasa or, even less, for the people of Tibet.

Before anyone rushes in to blame the Dalai Lama for giving his name and authority to such cynical malversation several things ought to be kept in mind. Firstly, he was largely isolated from his leading officials and advisers who, to all intents and purposes, were co-operating to a considerable extent with the Chinese. Secondly, he had seen the overwhelming strength of China during his visit there, had observed Nehru's close association with China, had experienced the disillusionment of having no help from the U.N., and had no accurate information on the strength

of the Kham and Amdo rebel forces. Thirdly, he had no knowledge of modern propaganda techniques and the possible effect his
reading of such a prepared speech would have on outside world
opinion; to him, it was obvious that the Tibetan people knew he
was under duress to attend such meetings and read such speeches,
and they would place no confidence in what was being said in the
light of that knowledge. It was unfortunate but, in the circumstances, understandable.

The propaganda not being of any use to the Chinese in Lhasa
itself, they had to take more concrete measures to keep matters
under their control. The Mi-mang Tsong-du stepped up their
activities in peaceful demonstrations and placarded the walls of
Lhasa with anti-Chinese leaflets. The Chinese then started a wave
of arrests.

One of the leaders of the Mi-mang Tsong-du, Alo Chondze, had
his house surrounded by Chinese troops armed with machine-
guns, and he was arrested without warning. Another two leaders,
Bhunthang Drunyee and Lapchuk, were also arrested and Lapchuk died in prison. Chinese troops in Lhasa increased to thirty-
five thousand and there were heavy concentrations of tanks and
armoured cars around the city. Food prices shot up as much as
thirty times the previous prices, due to the new influx of Chinese
personnel.

Also Chondze, the Mi-mang Tsong-du leader, managed to
escape from Lhasa to Kalimpong, and he and a Monk Commissioner of Gyantse, Tubthen Ningje, made full statements of conditions existing inside Tibet to the press and appealed for help.
According to them the fighting had spread from the Golok,
Batang and Litang areas to Nyarong, Taofu, Chatreng and Mili,
an area of some ten thousand square miles involving over two
million people. Bridges had been destroyed and the roads made
impassable for Chinese vehicles.

In August 1956 the Chinese authorities in Peking finally admitted that a rebellion had taken place in Tibet, or rather, in true
Chinese Communist fashion, they announced 'that there was no
rebellion but that fighting had taken place in some areas of
Western Szechuan'. The New China News Agency report stated

that 'A categorical denial of the rumoured rebellion in Tibet' had been made by Liu Ke-ping, a member of the Government concerned with the affairs of the minority nationalities in China. The report then went on to admit that Liu did, indeed, mention that there had been a 'rebellion' but claimed that the reports published in the West were based on 'distorted and grossly exaggerated delayed information'.

To begin with, the rebellion occurred 'not in Tibet, but in Western Szechuan—to be exact, in the Kanze autonomous district on the border of Tibet'. Secondly, 'it began many months ago, to be exact, around the end of February'. Thirdly, 'it was limited to the southern part of Kanze, which is far to the south of the Ya-an-Lhasa highway. Therefore reports that the highway had been cut by the rebels cannot be true'. (Actually, either this was a blatant misstatement by China in the hope that no one would know or care where Kanze was, or Liu himself was woefully ignorant, for Kanze is right on the Ya-an-Lhasa highway—even on Chinese Communist maps of the area.) Fourthly, it was provoked by Government reforms to restrict the landlords, and since the lamaseries and temples 'are being left outside the scope of these reforms . . . the "lamaist church" had no reason to take part in the rebellion and Western reports that it did are therefore wrong'. And, lastly, 'the rebellion has been settled in the main'.

Probably the real reason the Chinese made the hopeful claim that 'the rebellion has been settled in the main' was the lull in the fighting at that time due to the Chinese Prime Minister Chou En-lai's decision to send a 'Peace Mission' to Tibet to investigate the cause of the unrest. The Peace Mission had to report daily by wireless direct to Peking, and it was to submit its final reports and conclusions direct to the Prime Minister on its return to Peking.

At first the Peace Mission, under the leadership of Deputy Prime Minister Chen Yi, sought to negotiate with its own quisling Tibetans. The Kham and Amdo rebels refused to be represented by the Chinese hand-picked representatives of Ngabu and Karmapa, and demanded that their own Khamba leader, Topgyay Pangdatshang, represent their interests. They even sent a messenger to Kalimpong in July 1956 to ask Rapga Pangdatshang to return and represent them as their elected Governor of Markham, but Rapga was too astute and besides suspecting the Chinese intentions he felt he could do more for the Khambas by remaining outside Tibet. He did have personal talks with the Chinese Trade Agent in Kalimpong and the Chinese Consul-General in Calcutta.

In September the Deputy Prime Minister, Chen Yi, made his report on the visit to Tibet. He said that it had been agreed that Tibet should take the road to socialism. But it would be a long road and would have to be travelled slowly. Democratic reforms were to be carried out, but peacefully, and they were to leave room for guarantees for the 'political position and living standards of the Tibetan nobility and the lamas'. The State would support religious schools.

The November 6 issue of the Peking *Hsin Hua Pau Yueh Kau* (*New China Semi-monthly*) printed the speech of Chang Kuo-hua, Vice-Chairman of the Preparatory Committee for the Tibet Autonomous Region and Assistant-Secretary of the CCP Tibet Work Committee, at the Communist Party's Eighth Congress. In the course of his report it was obvious that the Peking authorities were being forced to move extremely cautiously in Tibet in order to consolidate their position.

'In the cause of bringing about autonomy in the nationality region', he said, 'training of nationality cadres is a basic problem of key importance. If there are insufficient numbers of Tibetan cadres with definite political understanding and working efficiency, all the work will encounter hardships difficult to overcome. In the past six years the cadres among both the ecclesiastical and the civil officials have attained definite and even great progress, and some two thousand one hundred new Tibetan cadres have been trained. However, the number of cadres and the rate of their growth are still lagging far behind the present demand and the work and party expansion have been insufficient. In order to expedite the growth of Tibetan cadres, cadre schools and training courses will be set up this year in Tibet, with the aim of recruiting from five to eight thousand Tibetan students in the coming four years, and training another ten thousand in rotation. In addition, large numbers of students will be sent to study in the Central

Institute for Nationalities, the South-west and the North-west Institution for Nationalities. . . .

'While deliberating on the question of social reform in Tibet it is necessary for us to take notice of the special conditions in that region. The policy, procedure and methods of reform in Tibet should not be the same as in the areas of Han nationality and other national minorities. Social reform in Tibet must not be implemented before and can only be carried out after conducting serious and repeated consultations with the upper-strata Tibetans until an overwhelming majority of these Tibetans genuinely approve and sponsor the reform and work out concrete methods to the satisfaction of the people of all strata and all circles. . . . The reason for the Party giving special consideration to the interests of the upper-strata Tibetans during and after the reforms is based on the concrete situation in Tibet. As the upper-strata Tibetans have intimate relations with the broad mass of the Tibetan people, as they have contributed much during the past several years in the unification of the motherland and the unity and progress of Tibet, and as these people themselves have already made various degrees of progress, the people of all the various nationalities throughout the country will not obliterate their merits and will have the justifiable reasons not to unite with them or take care of their interests, as long as the upper-strata Tibetans are willing to accept democratic and socialist reform. . . .'

On November 8 the Preparatory Office of the Tibet Committee of the Chinese People's Political Consultative Conference was set up in Lhasa with Chang Ching-wu, the representative of the Central People's Government, addressing the inaugural gathering. The Preparatory Office consisted of fifteen members, including Trichang Lobsang Yeshi, an assistant tutor to the Dalai Lama, Surkhang Wangchu Kaleh, director of the Office, and Puntshok Wangyel, former Batang Communist leader and number one collaborator, vice-director of the office.

Chang Ching-wu explained the nature and task of the Political Consultative Conference in detail, saying that the Tibet Committee of the CPPC was a local organization under the People's Democratic United Front led by the Chinese Communist Party, and that its task was to unite still more widely the various nationalities in Tibet, to help the Preparatory Committees for the Tibet Autonomous Region execute policies and decrees, and to strive to overcome difficulties and improve local construction. The establishment of this office, he concluded, was both a great political event and an important political task.

CHAPTER 14

The Dalai Lama's Agreement in India

While China was seeking to adjust its policies in Tibet to head off a nation-wide revolt the embassies in Peking and Delhi were busy seeking a solution to another Tibetan problem.

During his visit to China in 1954 the Indian Prime Minister, Mr. Nehru, had taken the opportunity to invite the Dalai Lama to pay a similar visit to India. As 1956 was to be the year of the Buddha Jayanti celebration in India, the 2,500th year since Buddha's attainment of Nirvana, it was thought appropriate that the Dalai Lama should visit India for the occasion.

It was certainly an excellent opportunity from India's point of view, coming at the time of Tibetan disillusion with China, but most inappropriate for China, which had no desire for the Dalai Lama to see what India or any other country was like and expose him to the possible effects of non-Communist interests. The Chinese were correspondingly cool to the suggestion, therefore, that the Dalai Lama should be permitted to go to India.

While the embassies exchanged notes the Maharaj Kumar of Sikkim, in his capacity of President of the Maha Bodhi Society, was commissioned to go to Lhasa with an invitation from the Maha Bodhi Society to the Dalai Lama to attend the Buddha Jayanti celebrations and at the same time to find out how the Dalai Lama would respond to an official invitation from the Indian Government. When it was known he was favourably disposed to this the official invitation was presented and the Dalai Lama officially accepted it. While the Chinese were reluctant to permit him to go to India, they were even more reluctant to provide any cause to the Tibetans to revolt again, and also to upset the amicable relations with India then prevailing.

On November 24 the Dalai Lama arrived in India. The Chinese had stipulated that the Panchen Lama would also have to be invited and he arrived at the same time as the Dalai Lama from Tibet.

There were tumultous scenes of welcome when the Dalai Lama entered India from Sikkim and the Tibetan residents of Kalimpong and Darjeeling gathered in their thousands to meet him. They had waited all night and when he finally appeared his car was surrounded by worshippers tossing the white ceremonial scarves. At the airfield of Bagdogra, where the plane was waiting to take the Dalai Lama and Panchen Lama to New Delhi, thousands broke through iron railings and police cordons before the aircraft could take off. The *shamiana* (marquee) in which they were seated was invaded by the surging crowds. An ugly incident involving injury to the Panchen Lama occurred when a stone tied in a ceremonial scarf struck him on the face. The security police hurried them both out of the shamiana into the airport restaurant, and closed all the doors and windows. The Dalai Lama was venerated and safe but with nearly ten thousand Tibetans convinced that the Panchen Lama was only a Chinese puppet anything might have happened.

At Delhi they were met by the Prime Minister, Mr. Nehru, and the Vice-President, Dr. Radhakrishnan, and about ten thousand cheering people. Both the Dalai Lama and Panchen Lama had brought with them retinues very much larger than any other visiting dignitary had ever brought to India. In addition to their immediate entourage of almost fifty people, another one hundred and fifty lamas and high officials were arriving independently to join in the celebration as India's guests.

Wherever he went the Dalai Lama charmed everyone he met, from the little five-year-old blonde girl, who gazed at him raptly while he smiled at her and stroked her cheek, to the most hardened newspapermen. He showed high intelligence as he asked surprisingly searching questions as, for instance, about the splitting of the atom or the pasteurization of milk.

The Panchen Lama was less vivacious and forthcoming. Like the Dalai Lama, he is a keen photographer, and he is passionately interested in electricity. He surprised his guides and interpreters at a reactor station with his informed questions on atomic energy.

A few days after their arrival in India China's Prime Minister, Chou En-lai, also arrived in India in the course of a tour through the countries of Asia. Chou was greeted in India with dignity, respect and hopefulness, for in addition to the admiration which most educated Indians had for China the success of India's foreign policy, 'The Five Principles of Peaceful Co-existence', depended on amity and co-operation between the two great countries of Asia. The importance of Tibet in his visit to India was indicated by the fact that an Indian expert on Tibet went with Chou everywhere throughout his Indian tour.

But it was not until Chou had left for Europe that the Dalai Lama made known to Mr. Nehru his startling decision that he was not going to return to Tibet. He asked Mr. Nehru for sanctuary in India for himself and the members of his Government, but if this was not possible then he wanted to request sanctuary in some other country. He had no intention of returning to Tibet.

This statement and others regarding subsequent discussions has been officially denied by Mr. Nehru in the Indian Parliament, but I was given the account by a member of the Dalai Lama's own family who also gave me permission to publish it after I had pointed out to him the possible repercussions. He was present at the time and during the following talks and was in a position to know all that went on. (This account was confirmed by the Dalai Lama in a public statement at a Press Conference on June 20, 1959.)

The Dalai Lama's decision was a considerable embarrassment to India for many reasons, not the least being that India had given assurances to China that the Dalai Lama's visit would not be an occasion for political intrigue. The Dalai Lama's outright refusal to return to Tibet in any circumstance left the Indian Government no room to manœuvre and Nehru had no option but to send word of the new development to Chou En-lai in Europe.

Chou returned for an unexpected three-day visit to India on his way back to China from Europe, and met the Dalai Lama and two of his brothers, Taktser Rimpoche and Gyalu Thondup, for private talks. Throughout the three-hour meeting Chou tried to persuade the Dalai Lama to return to Tibet with promises of reforms, a modification of the pace of reforms already introduced, and the punishment of local Chinese commanders who were guilty of atrocities, but the Dalai Lama remained adamant. He had heard too many Chinese promises and wanted no more of them. He would return to Tibet only when every Chinese had left his country.

Faced with this stalemate, Chou had to call in the Indian Prime Minister. At another private meeting, with Nehru present on this occasion, both Prime Ministers tried to alter the Dalai Lama's decision. Finally, when Nehru agreed to see that Chou's assurances of China's withdrawal from Tibet were implemented and undertook that he himself would pay a visit to Lhasa later in the year to see the situation for himself, the Dalai Lama agreed to return to Tibet.

A minor point of controversy discussed at the meeting, whether the Dalai Lama should visit the controversial border town of Kalimpong, which Chou was very much against, was used as a reason for the discussions to cover the more important intransigence of the Dalai Lama. Even this minor point Chou had to concede, for the Dalai Lama insisted on visiting Kalimpong where so many of his faithful followers were waiting.

After Chou's return to Peking political observers there reported a change in the attitude of Communist China's leading officials towards India. There was distrust of India's new *rapprochement* with the United States following on Nehru's visit and talks with President Eisenhower. There was a recognized lack of progress and accomplishment, from Peking's point of view, in the recent talks between Chou En-lai and Prime Minister Nehru. And there was a growing conviction that the co-existence policy with India had been far more rewarding for India than it had for China.

When Chou En-lai was approached, shortly after his return to Peking, about rumours that the Dalai Lama and Panchen Lama had been contacted by United States agents in efforts to influence them against returning to their Chinese-controlled country, he admitted knowledge of such rumours. When asked what policy China would pursue if the two Lamas did not return, and if there was a national uprising, the Premier announced that Peking would be forced to adopt the policy that she had already endorsed in Hungary.

However, the Dalai Lama and the Panchen Lama both returned to Tibet in January 1957. But before doing so the Dalai Lama requested and obtained permission to leave behind in India another brother, Lobsang Samten, and a trusted minister, Lukhangwa. Lobsang Samten, after receiving medical treatment for a few months, slipped away quietly to join his brother, Taktser Rimpoche, in America, but Lukhangwa remained in Kalimpong to keep in touch with the situation in Tibet.

CHAPTER 15

Chinese Violation of Agreement

The Dalai Lama returned to Lhasa and was received with great pomp and circumstance by the Chinese occupation personnel. There was no doubt that the Chinese policy was to placate the Tibetans as much as possible and to ride out what they hoped was only a temporary storm.

However, it was not long before they succumbed to the temptation to indulge in some political finaigling at the expense of naïve Tibetan officialdom. After reducing the promise of 'Chinese withdrawal from Tibet' to 'reduction of certain Han personnel in various offices in the autonomous Tibet region of China' they also altered one significant part of the agreement which read 'withdrawal . . . being the will of the Tibetan people' to read 'reduction . . . being the will of the Tibetan people and officials'. They then proceeded to work on certain of the Tibetan officials individually to renounce their expressed 'will' for Chinese withdrawal, and the Tibetan officials were only too happy to agree in order not to be blamed for their outspoken claims while in India.

It was only a step from this to the Chinese claim that it was not the will of the Tibetan officials that they should leave Tibet. Further, the agreement to reduce Han personnel in Tibet applied only to that area west of Gyamda Dzong and not to the area of Szechuan east of Gyamda Dzong which was China proper, and the rebel elements still in that area would have to surrender or be suitably punished.

The Khambas were stunned at this announcement, first of all at the betrayal implicit in the Lhasa officials' statement and then, after all their sacrifices, at the explicit claim that they were not to be recognized as Tibetans but Chinese. The bitter feeling against the Lhasa Government and everything it stood for crystallized into hatred and the Kham and Amdo Tibetans swore that when the time came they would kill every Lhasa official with the Chinese. This feeling was exacerbated by a fresh spate of gun-running following on the Tibetan officials' visit to India and their establishment of private contacts with arms suppliers there. The Lhasa officials who had been able to arrange for supplies then proceeded to amass large profits by charging the desperate Khambas extortionate prices for guns and ammunition, prices being as high as £300 for a rifle and £3–5 for a bullet.

In Lhasa the Chinese Communist-controlled *Si Tsang Jih Pao* (Tibet Daily) of August 2 carried the following 'Outline of Propaganda for CCP Tibet Working Committee Concerning the Policy of not implementing Democratic Reform in Tibet Within Six Years'.

'After the resolution of implementing democratic reforms in Tibet was suggested and passed last year at the inaugural meeting of the Preparatory Committee for introducing Regional Autonomy in Tibet, facts have proved that only a few of the upper-strata personages support it, while the majority still harbour varying degrees of doubt and are actually against it; and that although a small portion of the masses enthusiastically demand reforms, the large portion of the masses still lack such enthusiasm. On this account, conditions for the reform are still inadequate at present. In order to give consideration to the above-mentioned actual conditions and benefits concerning the strengthening of unity among nationalities, the Central Committee has decided not to implement the democratic reform in Tibet during the period of the Second Five Year Plan. As to whether the democratic reform will be implemented during the Third Five Year Plan period or not, the question will be decided according to the actual conditions in Tibet then. . . .

'In view of the fact that there will be "no reform in six years", the present organs and personnel—particularly Han cadres—of the Tibet Autonomy Preparatory Committee are far too many. Originally Han cadres were transferred here to help the Tibetan people make preparations for the democratic reform. In the past year they and the Tibetan cadres helped each other, learned from each other, and united and closely co-operated with each other. Since it has now been decided that there will be "no reform in six years", most of these Han cadres have no work to do any more, and they of course should be transferred to other parts of the motherland to participate in various socialist undertakings. However, in order to continue helping the Tibetan people to proceed with certain constructive projects, it is still necessary to leave a certain number of Han cadres in Tibet, according to such requirements. . . .

'Last year, while making preparations for democratic reforms, we made proper political and economic arrangements for some of the upper-level personages. Since there will be "no reform in six years" there will be no change in the original income of these upper-level personages, and therefore the state, in principle, should not continue to issue salaries to these personages. However, those who cannot be spared should remain at their posts and continue to receive pay. Proper assistance should be rendered to patriotic personages who really have livelihood difficulties. . . .

'Last year a number of schools were opened in various places in Tibet. This has a positive function in the development of cultural and educational undertakings in Tibet and the training of skilled persons for building up Tibet. However, certain upper-level personages are even dissatisfied with our opening schools. At the same time the unreasonable phenomenon of drafting people into schools appeared in certain localities, arousing many complaints from the students' parents. From now on the schools in various places should be readjusted according to the principle of voluntariness and should be, in the main, operated by local authorities of Tibet. . . .

'The Central Government's decision to postpone any reform in Tibet for six years is made according to the actual situation where only a minority of the upper-strata Tibetans support the reform while the majority are against it. From now on People's Liberation Army units and working personnel stationed in Tibet will con-

tinue to faithfully implement the agreement on the peaceful liberation of Tibet, strengthen unity with the people of Tibet of all
strata, assist the Tibetan people to do all beneficial things which
can be done, and strive for the consolidation of the unity of the
motherland as well as our national defence and internal security.
If any imperialist element or any separationist takes the opportunity of our reduction of our establishment, or under any pretext
in the future, to try to conduct sabotaging activities and manufacture revolts, then we will give him this solemn warning: we are
determined to implement the agreement on the peaceful liberation
of Tibet; but if someone dares to violate any one of the Seventeen
Articles of the agreement and manufacture revolts, then the
People's Liberation Army has the responsibility to suppress the
revolt; by that time the People's Liberation Army will certainly
join hands with all patriotic citizens in dealing firm and telling
blows to the rebellious elements. . . .'

One week later, on August 8, the CCP Tibet Working Committee announced that by the end of July organs and units under their
jurisdiction had already sent away 91·6 per cent of the Han cadres
and workers, as well as Tibetan cadres.

However, in October there were still stray undercurrents of revolt, particularly in Kham. Chang Kuo-hua, the Assistant-Secretary of the CCP Tibet Working Committee, used the occasion of
the first anniversary of the founding of the Chinese Buddhist
Association in Tibet to warn the Tibetans. After the usual Communist preamble eulogizing the activities of the Party and Chairman Mao, he listed three types of religious people in Tibet who
held different viewpoints. The first category comprised those who
loved their mother-country passionately and who wanted above
all socialism and unity with the great motherland of China. The
second category consisted of people who were incessantly raising
their own political consciousness and were generally in favour of
the principle of delaying reform for six years. While recognizing
that the road to socialism was indispensable they still cherished
doubts and worries about future reform in Tibet and freedom of
religious belief. The third category was of people who fell prey to
the rumours of the imperialist and reactionary elements and

adopted certain non-patriotic attitudes. He indicated that the third category was still very much in the majority.

In India the Indian Government had asked Lukhangwa, the former Prime Minister of Tibet left behind to represent the Dalai Lama, to prepare a Memorandum on the situation in Tibet, which presented a far different picture. Here are some extracts:

'Having been hit hard by the stubborn resistance of the Tibetan people, the Chinese have now resorted to the well-known colonial policy of "divide and rule". In this endeavour they have boosted their own puppets to raise the slogan of rivalry among different people and parts of the country. They have also brought about a change in the original set-up of the country and thus Ü, Tsang and Kham are created as distinct constituents. In this manner they have started rifts between the Khamba and a man from Ü (i.e. Lhasa area) and again between a Lhasa man and a Tsang man (i.e. a person from Shigatse, farther south). These rifts and rivalries are being encouraged to divert the Tibetan mind from their national sentiments, thus producing a psychological effect which paves the way for more subversive activities. . . .

'They have robbed us of our privacy and domestic life. The Chinese, whether civilian or soldier, enter our houses and private chambers without permission. In the inner parts of the country they even break open doors, whether locked or bolted, and make themselves comfortable and at home without even enquiring about the master of the house or the head of the family. In contrast the Tibetans are not even allowed to look towards the Chinese establishments, residences, hospitals or forts. . . .

'In order to calm or pacify the people's opposition, the Peking Government agreed to postpone "the great march to socialism" for a period of six years. Ostensibly to fulfil their promise, the Chinese have abandoned the construction of buildings and defence projects in the town and populated areas, and have returned some of the civilians—i.e. forced labourers, technicians, engineers and such. To keep a firm hold on the country they have augmented their armed forces so that they are ten times stronger than before. They have become more oppressive inasmuch as they lay their hands on many innocent Tibetans with murderous intentions. Last year on the occasion of a festival called "Sebang" a Chinese soldier equipped with hand-grenades reached even to the premises of the Dalai Lama's chambers, but was subsequently overpowered by the Dalai Lama's loyal guards. When the culprit was handed over to the Chinese no enquiry was made about this dangerous action by one of their own men. There is no freedom of expression or even movement to a Tibetan. The Tibetans cannot even gather for social and religious functions. . . .

'In a nutshell it may be said that the Chinese in those (Kham) areas of Tibet are trying their utmost to rob the Tibetans of their loyalty to the Dalai Lama's Government, their faith in the traditions and religion of the land, and their deep sense of attachment to the country's cultural heritage. It is in view of these facts and sentiments that Don-Kham, the eastern region of Tibet, is today the main centre of revolt against the Communists. Taking Don-Kham as a whole the main tribes of fighters hail from different tribal areas. They belong to regions stretching due east like Lithang, Charteng, Lingkar-Shiba, Batang, Gyalthang, Derge, Nyarong, Horko and Golok. The Chinese have not spared any means to subdue these patriot strongholds. They have mobilized thousands of armed forces, well-equipped with the latest weapons. The partisans have been inflicted with air attacks with gas as well as explosive bombs. . . . Devastation and destruction of the natural resources of the country are widespread. In their hectic struggle to assimilate the Tibetans culturally and to dominate them ideologically the Chinese have used the savage means of destroying the centres of worship. . . .

'It is for these reasons that thousands of young Tibetans are still fighting hard against Chinese rule. These guerrilla forces are hiding in the deserts and forests of those eastern Kham territories. While rebellion persists in these areas of Kham the Chinese have actually started a reign of terror upon innocent children and womenfolk who can neither fight nor escape atrocities. . . . On the pretext of their being "malcontents" people were sent far into the inner regions to build roads and highways, and in winter they were used as slave labour to clear snow from the highway. They became snow-blinded, bruised physical misfits. As to the aged or "useless" persons, the Chinese are absolutely indifferent. Having no means of making a living, not even being allowed to beg, hundreds died for want of food. Many others could not stand the cruel treatment and resorted to suicide by jumping from the mountain tops and falling into the rivers. . . .

'The Tibetans are seriously watching the next move of the invaders. They have not taken lightly the repeated warnings that the Chinese are inclined to give our people with regard to the launching of the "big step" to Socialism. Our people are suffering an uncertain future with all the accompanying possibilities of assimilation, infiltration and domination of a colonial power with an ideology completely foreign to our genius. In spite of all the opposition and resistance, the Chinese seem to be bent on bringing about the change, and what the average Tibetan—fighter and partisan—is wondering is what will be the ultimate result of such changes. If these changes were brought about and Tibet became absorbed by the Chinese it would be difficult to imagine the final picture. . . .'

CHAPTER 16

Revolt Spreads Westwards

At the beginning of 1958 the Khamba and Amdo guerrillas had disrupted over five hundred miles of roads between Chungking and Lhasa, and they were operating as far westwards as the town of Gyamda Dzong, only a hundred and sixty miles east of Lhasa. Whole towns had changed hands several times as the fighting fluctuated, and one large garrison town between Gyamda Dzong and Chamdo, with over six thousand Chinese troops and five thousand civilians employed on road repairs, had to be abandoned because of guerrilla activity.

Chinese Communists, in addition to the few 'Han cadres' withdrawn, had also transferred some of their troops stationed in West Tibet—where Indian observers could report that the Chinese were apparently keeping to the letter of their agreement to withdraw—to East Tibet where they were supplemented by other troops from China to make an active force of over a hundred thousand in order to clear up the rebels. Air attacks with high explosive bombs, gas and napalm bombs were used. But even against this formidable attack the Khambas cleared the whole of the mountainous area formed by the triangle of Derge, Batang and Litang, with other pockets in Amdo and South Kham. One guerrilla leader who arrived in Kalimpong from this area told me that they had already killed over forty thousand Chinese since the fighting began in 1956. No casualties were taken or tended, for the Tibetans were using fast riding marauding tactics to outfight the Chinese and could not take care of wounded.

The Chinese authorities in Lhasa became increasingly concerned with the spread of the revolt, and in Lhasa itself they introduced a reorganization of the Tibetan Army to diminish the possibility of an uprising from amongst the many Khambas in its ranks. From a total of twenty thousand they had quietly shed five thousand before the Tibetans found out the manœuvre and refused to be depleted further. The Lhasa garrison force was kept at five thousand, all faithful to the Dalai Lama and under trusted commanders. Another move by the Chinese to destroy the growing spirit of nationalism was the attempt to replace the Tibetan flag with the Chinese, and even to hoist the Chinese Communist emblem on the Potala where no flag had ever flown, but this too had to be foregone in the face of intense Tibetan protests.

About this time 'unofficial' reports began circulating in Delhi that Mr. Nehru would soon visit Tibet in response to the invitation extended to him by the Dalai Lama during his visit to India. This news was picked up by Tibetans in India and relayed to Lhasa where it was received with jubilation. For if Mr. Nehru visited Lhasa he would see for himself the military occupation and oppression of the Chinese and the antipathy the Tibetans felt towards them, and as a just and humane man he must respond to Tibetan appeals for help.

But it was in East Tibet that the Chinese pursued their ruthless policy of extermination. At Langra, in Amdo, the Chinese used the famous leader, Geshi Sherab Gyaltso, to persuade the Tibetans in that area to make an oath on their scriptures, the Kangyur, to give up resistance and hand over their arms, in return for which the Chinese would guarantee their safety. A month later the Chinese mercilessly killed fifteen hundred unarmed men and women. Within a year Geshi Sherab Gyaltso was to atone for his mistake by making a passionate public speech, confessing his error and denouncing the Chinese—and he then disappeared.

In the Golok area the Chinese staged a reign of terror to try finally to intimidate these fierce tribesmen, killing thousands and destroying hundreds of monasteries. The Golok Rimpoche was put to death by boiling water being poured over his head. Other high lamas suffered equally grim tortures, while hundreds more jumped into the River Ma-chu to drown rather than be captured. In Jyekundo many monasteries were razed to the ground by air attacks. A famous lama, Lab Sonam Tsemo, was burnt to death and thousands of men and women were killed, either in the fighting or by torture following on their capture. In Derge the Chinese destroyed over two hundred and fifty monasteries, including the famous Dzokchen and Derge monasteries containing priceless manuscripts and treasures. Well-known lamas were dragged to death behind their horses, and famous Tibetan leaders were taken bound down-country to China.

To eliminate the religion the Chinese issued a pamphlet rationalizing the Tibetan religious beliefs. In the pamphlet Buddha was depicted as a fugitive from his own country because of the revolt of his subjects against his unjust rule. In order to subdue them, the Communists stated, he had concocted a religion to hoodwink them into obedience, which religion became known as Buddhism. Later the Chinese tried to recover this dangerous pamphlet from circulation and even offered five Chinese dollars for every one recovered.

At the same time China was pouring a reputed three to five million 'colonizers' into East Tibet in a systematic and ruthless programme of absorption and annihilation of the Tibetan people. Starting in the open plateaux of Amdo, and some areas of Kham, they occupied valley after valley, forcing the few remaining to take in Chinese settlers and look after them, fathering children on the Tibetan women, and then moving more colonists into the next valley, and so on. The brutal repression of the guerrillas caused less concern amongst the Kham and Amdo Tibetans than this enforced colonization programme, and what had been a steady infiltration to the mountains of young and able-bodied Tibetans spoiling for a fight became a mass exodus of all Tibetans able to walk.

At the beginning of April 1958, at a Party meeting in Lhasa, the Chinese launched an all-out purge of 'liberals', 'deviationists' and 'counter-revolutionary elements' amongst military, official and civilian personnel. In the purge the leading Tibetan Communist, Puntshok Wangyel, who had been a Party member for over twenty years and who had led the Chinese Communists into Tibet in 1950, was arrested for protesting against the Chinese reform programme with the accompanying atrocities. He also advocated that Tibet should become a fully autonomous region in the Chinese Republic without undue interference from Peking. After his arrest he was taken to China, where he disappeared. Over five thousand Chinese were arrested in the purge, one thousand and sixty-eight of them in Lhasa alone.

Yet with all the momentous implications of revolt in Tibet, the desperate struggles of a nation facing genocide, it was impossible to get a line of print into the world's press. I bombarded newspapers and journals in Britain and America only to have the articles politely returned. With all the courteous wording of the rejection it was obvious that no one believed what I wrote of the situation in Tibet.

The London *Times* carried a long article that caused dismay amongst the Tibetan community in India. The writer claimed that Tibet was happy with Chinese occupation, sang cheerfully the Communist songs, had a rising standard of living and preferred Mao Tse-tung's photograph to the Dalai Lama's.

The *Statesman* correspondent sent several reports, meticulously cross-checked, to his paper but none of them was printed.

The *Daily Telegraph* at this juncture cabled me asking for everything I could give on the revolt and at last what was happening in Tibet began to circulate throughout the world. This evoked a response in Indian official circles, which issued a frigid denial that anything untoward was happening in Tibet.

On August 4 the *Manchester Guardian* correspondent in New Delhi reported:

'Stories of large-scale rioting and massacre in Tibet reported in a section of the press, particularly abroad, are regarded in official circles as grossly exaggerated.

'Apparently all of the stories have come from Tibetan *émigrés* who have settled down in Kalimpong and other towns on the Indian side of the border. The Chinese Government had already drawn the attention of the Indian Government to the unfriendly campaign. Some of the *émigrés* who have been forwarding periodically memoranda on the situation in Tibet have been warned by the Indian Government not to indulge in anti-Chinese activities on Indian soil.

'Some of the Tibetans presumably think that India has continued to have a special say in the internal developments in Tibet, as it had before the emergence of the present Chinese Government in Peking. Some of them still harp on the idea of independence for Tibet and have been unable to reconcile themselves to the new situation.

'Apparently the Chinese are now engaged in correcting the "revisionists".'

Inside Tibet events had moved irrevocably to a national crisis. An estimated two hundred thousand Chinese troops were occupied in an all-out war of extermination in East Tibet. The Kham and Amdo rebels had withdrawn where possible into inaccessible mountain areas where the Chinese could not follow them, and where this was not possible had begun to fall back westwards on Lhasa.

In June between twelve and fifteen thousand of the rebels had entered Lhasa and created a major problem for the Chinese Communist authorities as they increased the tension already high in Lhasa. The Chinese ordered the Lhasa Government to send all their 'refugees' back to the 'East Tibetan Autonomous Region' to be dealt with by the authorities there, but then an unexpected occurrence took place.

While not defying the Chinese outright the Lhasa Government delayed taking any open decision. Gradually the Kham and Amdo rebels secretly left Lhasa, with supplies of food and arms, for the surrounding mountains. By mid-July twenty-three groups of Tibetans totalling about twenty thousand were fighting in the south and south-western areas of Tibet. Another thirty thousand were fighting in Markham in the south-east and thirty thousand in Amdo.

The Lhasa officials had at last committed themselves to join the East Tibetans in their revolt against the Chinese and make it a national uprising.

In Lhasa some of the East Tibetan rebel leaders had been in touch with leading officials of the Tibetan Government, and had decided that as a token of their new unity of purpose the old name given to the rebels, Chu-Zhi Kang-Druk (Four Rivers, Six Snow

Mountains), a slogan based on an early name for Tibet, should be dropped in favour of a new one, Chul-ka Sum. Chul-ka Sum was an ancient name for Tibet derived from the three major provinces, Kham, Amdo and Ü-Tsang. With the introduction of the new name the Tibetan people would know that it was no longer a Kham and Amdo uprising but a revolt of all the people of Tibet against the Chinese aggressors. At the same time messengers were sent to Kalimpong to Tibetan exile officials to organize Tibetans living in the border areas in India into a Chul-ka Sum group there and to do what they could to obtain and send help to Tibet.

On August 1, after a meeting in Kalimpong, sixteen groups of Tibetans toured Gangtok, Kalimpong, Darjeeling and Kurseong collecting signatures of loyalty to the new nationalist movement. Everyone who did not sign or give some concrete indication of help for their beleaguered countrymen inside Tibet was to be considered a traitor. From the members of the Dalai Lama's family through Cabinet Ministers, local union officials to the lowliest Tibetan coolie in the bazaar, all Tibetans rushed to sign. Only two Tibetans of note did not sign, one of them pleading sickness and the other, Rapga Pangdatshang, refusing outright because, he maintained, there was no guarantee of a change of government, no Kham and Amdo representation, and no Dalai Lama and Lhasa Government seal.

Hoarded guns, money, horses, mules and three hundred young Tibetans were collected and sent to the rebel forces fighting in Tibet. The Chinese moved to counteract this and put renewed pressure on the Indian Government to return all Tibetan exiles in India to Tibet. The Indian Government did not accede to this request but warned the leading Tibetans, as already indicated, that they must not indulge in political activities or they would be sent out of the country.

On the evening of August 4, 1958, every Tibetan official of note in India, including the Dalai Lama's brother and their Cabinet Ministers, together with guerrilla leaders as delegates from the fighting rebels, met in Kalimpong to draw up a final appeal to India and the United Nations. The extreme guerrilla rebel elements wanted to take some immediate action such as attacking Sikkim or Bhutan in order to publicize their predicament and at the same time obtain the desperately needed food for the starving people inside Tibet, but the moderate elements amongst the Tibetan officials had made a last try to head off the extremists by suggesting an appeal to the United Nations.

By midnight, August 4, the Appeal and Manifesto was drawn up. On the morning of August 5 over three hundred were posted to countries represented on the United Nations, responsible newspapers, and religious organizations throughout the world.

The Appeal and Manifesto read:

'Dear Sir, Tibet is essentially an independent country with sovereign powers. Its people being religious and peace-loving, no stock of modern war-weapons was kept within its boundaries. In the year 1950 the Chinese Communists invaded our land with about five hundred thousand of their so-called "liberation army" and overpowered our frontier guards. Later they settled some four million Chinese immigrants in the eastern and north-eastern regions. These settlers, along with their powerful armies, have attempted to destroy our religion, culture and traditions.

'We Tibetans, both in Tibet and in India, have tried our utmost to make the Chinese recognize their shameful injustice to us and we have asked them several times to stop the oppression and suppression of our people. We have also approached you, Mr. Nehru, in the past, asking you to use your influence with the Chinese on our behalf, but all these efforts proved vain. We have already explained the Tibetan situation to you and know that you are well aware of the facts. In spite of this we are attaching hereto a Manifesto describing the plight of our people. In it you will read of the merciless treatment of our people by the Chinese, and how many had to flee to the far-off deserts and valleys. It is for these reasons that our people are now fighting for freedom. There are hundreds being killed daily by the Chinese in these battles.

'There is trouble also in Lhasa, the capital of Tibet. Recently some thirty-thousand people from the southern areas had to leave their property, families and settled life to save themselves from the brutal treatment of the Chinese overlords. Now without homes, these people are also out in the deserts and it is feared that there may be uprisings in the south and central areas as a consequence.

'Not only have the Chinese Communists occupied our country and set about exploiting our people, but they also made Tibet into a huge arsenal for their future offensive towards her neighbouring countries and the world at large. They are building army barracks, forts, bridges, airfields at strategic places and their immense programme for constructing great roads and railways is mainly to accelerate the movement of their armed forces.

'It is in view of the above-mentioned facts and because of your close and cordial relations with China that we request you kindly to make the Government of China realize the desperate situation in our country. We request you to endeavour to make the Chinese immediately stop their offensive which they are launching against the patriots in Don-Kham and Amdo in the eastern regions, and to make the situation in central Tibet easier.

'India, a country which was under British domination for over a hundred and fifty years, achieved her independence just after the World War II. Similarly a number of other countries which were under foreign yokes for generations have attained their independence within the past few years. On the contrary, the independence of Tibet, an essentially free country which, as history proves, was at no time under any foreign domination, was violated by Communist China, her next-door neighbour. Can the peace-loving countries of the world justify the atrocious actions of the Chinese Communists in Tibet while its people are fighting tooth and nail in a struggle for their very existence?

'Since yours is a country which prizes its freedom, we look to you to do what you can to help. Therefore our appeal to you is this. Please request the Government of China on our behalf to allow Tibet to regain her independence and to withdraw all their armed forces and immigrants from the whole of Tibet.'

MANIFESTO TO THE UNITED NATIONS FROM THE
TIBETAN CHUL-KA-SUM, AUGUST 5, 1958

After a lengthy historical introduction the Manifesto went on:
'Tibet, independent and peace-loving, has a theocratic form of

Government with His Holiness the Dalai Lama as its sole ruler. Its language, culture, traditions are completely different from those of China. Yet, in the year 1949, when the Communists subdued the whole of China, they declared to the whole world through the radio that China wanted to "liberate" Tibet.

'The Chinese suddenly attacked the eastern regions of our country from eight different directions. Being a non-violent and peace-loving country, Tibet had no stock of arms and ammunition, and the legal Government of the country approached the United Nations General Assembly for justice and to check the further advance of the Chinese invasion. Receiving no reply from that Assembly, we approached the Security Council at its session at Lake Success. To our greatest disappointment both of our appeals were ignored and remain unanswered to this day. It was under these circumstances that the Chinese forced our Governor at Chamdo to submit to their dictates and to make the Government of Lhasa surrender. To the Governor was dictated the so-called "Seventeen-Point Agreement", which he had to translate into Tibetan. Then he was forced to sign it on behalf of the Government of Tibet by the threat of further troops being sent into Tibet if this was not done. No document is legal without the official seal of the Cabinet duly sanctioned by the Dalai Lama, but the Chinese made a seal of their own for the purpose (and this seal is still in their possession); therefore the agreement was never properly signed.

'Since that time the Tibetans have suffered untold agonies. The Chinese Communists have gradually deprived us of all our political rights. Our Government, right from the top to the provincial and district offices, has been made powerless and today we are governed completely by the Chinese. Soon after their occupation in 1951 the Chinese organized the Regional Military Commanders and abolished our National Army, and the Commanders and Vice-Commanders of our own forces were enlisted with the Communists' forces to bring them into line with the forces of occupation. During 1953–54 the Chinese tried to establish their Military and Political Committee to abolish the Tibetan Government. But the bitter opposition of the people prevented this. By the end of

1954 the Chinese managed to take the Dalai Lama to China and there he was forced to agree and confirm that the autonomous state of Tibet would submit to the establishment of the Regional Autonomous Government of Tibet. In 1955 the Dalai Lama returned to Tibet. In 1956 the Chinese, in order to consolidate their hold on Tibet, formed the preparatory committee of the Regional Autonomous Government of Tibet. This Committee is directly governed by the Peking Government. All its members, both Chinese and Tibetans, must be approved by the Peking authorities and all its decisions must first be confirmed by them. They have installed their own agents in that Committee with fifty-fifty representation of Chinese and Tibetans, and have used those Tibetan puppets to influence the decisions of the Committee. Thus politically the Tibetans have been made completely subservient to the Chinese overlords.

'Economically Tibet used to be self-sufficient in its food supply. But today millions of Chinese are living on our people and our food situation is desperate. The people in the east and north-east are facing a famine. The Chinese, besides laying hands on our current crops, have forced our people to open our centuries-old granaries. They have also taken away our reserves of gold and silver bullion. In the southern and central regions they have destroyed thousands of acres of agricultural land by giving priority to "national highways" and to the building of barracks and arsenals. In the east and north-east regions the Chinese have introduced the Communist method of land reforms. In these areas half the population are peasants and the other half nomads. To effect their land reforms the Chinese have imported masses of their settlers and distributed the agricultural land of the Tibetans among them. They have in this way introduced the collectivization of farms. In this process the Chinese have made the despoiled Tibetan farmers work twelve hours a day, with a daily ration insufficient for a single meal. In the distribution of property they have not even spared the Tibetans' personal requisites of everyday life, such as rugs, rooms in the houses and articles of clothing. Our Tibetans are expected to treat these Chinese settlers as their aunts and uncles, and share all their property equally with the immigrants. The nomads too are victims of these so-called reforms. Their flocks of sheep and cattle, their wool and dairy products are all being confiscated by the alien Government.

'In the name of education they have opened schools of various denominations, organized training centres such as a "Youth League", "Women's Association", and "Workers' Party", and they are trying their utmost to enlist as many as possible of our young men and children. In this way they have made thousands of homes unhappy by sending their children to China for the so-called advancement of their education. None of these children is being trained or educated for any constructive purposes. There are no Tibetan engineers, electricians, chemists or doctors. They train our youths to distrust each other. They are trying to indoctrinate the young Tibetans' minds and to strengthen the forces of Communism in our land. As a result they have divided families: son against father, wife against husband, thus alienating Tibetans from their own culture, tradition and homeland.

'In the matter of religion they have their own schemes to subvert the very bases of Buddha's Teachings. Our religion teaches love for all and malice for none. The Communists in their struggle to spread the Marxist ideology have used our well-known monk scholars to mislead the simple Tibetans. In this endeavour they made Geyshey Sherab Gyatso, one of the well-known monk scholars, propagate their own doctrine by writing pamphlets and translating their various books and articles. They have also used the Panchen Lama as a puppet to advance their political purposes in Tibet. Pamphlets and articles of propaganda have been spread all over Tibet since 1948–58, and Communism is being preached to all our people. In Kumbum (one of the famous monasteries in the east) the Chinese have actually made our head lamas study Marxist Dialectics. Ordinary monks they try to overcome by such material arguments as this: the monks are made to remain in their cells and try to procure food by prayer alone. If the food is not miraculously produced, this is supposed to prove that God does not exist. Meantime the Communists prevent the monks from using their God-given natural powers to procure food, and torture them by hunger into abandoning their simple faith. The

Communists preach day in and day out to our simple people and monks that religion is nothing short of an opium to distract the human mind from hard work. They have used hundreds of these monks as labourers in the building of roads and barracks. They have stopped the monasteries from sharing the usual food reserves and thousands of monks starved to death for this reason. They have forced many of our monks to marry and move to China to earn a living. They have laid hands on the capital of these monasteries and even subjected to tax the very idols and statues. Such has been the battle of Marxist Ideology against our spiritual heritage.

'Outwardly they are telling people that they have come to Tibet to protect and help the Tibetans and to build roads, hospitals and airfields. As a matter of fact the roads are being built to connect Tibet with the Chinese mainland in order to transport millions of their armed forces to the far-flung areas of Tibet. In making these thousands of miles of roads they have used Tibetans as forced labourers and thousands of them have died for want of food and proper care. Their hospitals are not meant for these poor victims but are mainly to use for their armed forces. The Tibetans even in the towns are not allowed to use these army hospitals. The big airfields that they have built are mainly for the purpose of bringing in fuel, arms and ammunition. Tibetans are not even allowed to pass near those airfields guarded so heavily by our oppressor. All these constructions are mainly for the purpose of consolidating their hold on Tibet and to suppress and preserve the conquered land and people of Tibet.

'To us Tibetans the phrase "the liberation of Tibet", in its moral and spiritual implication, is a deadly mockery. The country of a free people was invaded and occupied under the pretext of liberation . . . liberation from whom and what? Ours was a happy country with solvent Government and a contented people till the Chinese invasion in 1950.

'In view of all these facts the Tibetans approached the Chinese with a view to conciliation. But all our efforts went in vain. Instead we are subjected to untold cruelty. The people of eastern Tibet revolted against the Chinese in February 1956. These spontaneous uprisings brought about further repression by the conquerors. They have desecrated religious buildings and destroyed monasteries, razed villages to the ground and killed thousands of our people. They have also used poison gas. Bombs have been thrown on innocent children and women. More than fifteen thousand people have been injured in these battles. Life in all parts of Tibet has become unbearable. So much so that more than thirty thousand people in central Tibet round about Lhasa, the capital, left their hearth and home for the far-off valleys and gorges. It is feared that trouble may also flare up in these areas. Many places in Kham and Amdo are still scenes of upheaval and turmoil. Our patriots are fighting hard in these areas. Some of the Amdos who fled to the mountains are still not giving up their fight for freedom, suffering at least a hundred casualties a day.'

India moved swiftly to counteract the effect of this unprecedented Appeal and the Tibetans were warned that no further such statements must be issued or they would be given twenty-four hours to leave the country. Further, no statements were to be given to newspaper correspondents who might come looking for news. At first this warning was only given to the signatories of the Appeal but within a few days it was extended to include twenty-five leading Tibetans in Kalimpong and Darjeeling.

However, copies of the Appeal and Manifesto had been sent to two Indian leaders who had always expressed sympathy for Tibet, Jayaprakash Narayan and Acharya Kripalani, and both made the matter a subject of public comment. In a speech in India's Lok Sabha, Kripalani said: 'Perhaps I will not be misunderstood when I say that this great doctrine (Panch Shila) was born in sin, because it was enunciated to put the seal of our approval upon the destruction of an ancient nation which was associated with us spiritually and culturally. The Panch Shila was annunciated on the eve of a nation losing its liberty.'

In his reply Prime Minister Nehru, repeating Acharya Kripalani's remark that Panch Shila was born in sin, said that according to the Christian doctrine we were all born in sin. From a purely practical point of view there was no other course open to India,

12. The ferry boat at Ramagang, on the River Kyi, where the Dalai Lama escaped down river from Lhasa to join the Khamba guerrillas in the mountains (and to safety)

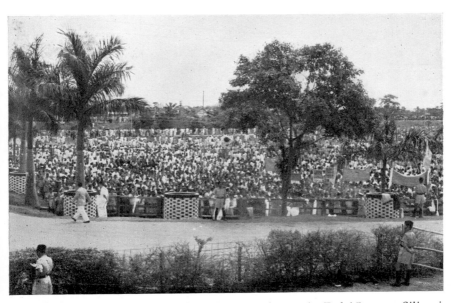

13. A section of the huge crowd waiting to welcome the Dalai Lama at Siliguri, after his dramatic escape from Lhasa. The banners are in English, Hindu and Tibetan

14. Topgyay Pangdatshang with one of his sons; Topgyay, although leader of the Khambas, is held under strict Chinese Communist supervision in Chamdo. The rebel fighter, Andrutshang, was in touch with him secretly during the fighting but there was little that Topgyay could do to help from his position in Chamdo.

15. Some of the leading Tibetan Government officials in India waiting to greet the Dalai Lama on his arrival. The Indian police in the foreground kept them from approaching the Dalai Lama, or even the railway platform, for what were more political than security reasons. Centre foreground is Shakabpa, former Minister of Finance, and behind his left shoulder, Tethong, both intimately concerned in the revolt

he maintained. India could not have challenged China's action over Tibet in 1950.

Whatever India may have thought of China's friendship and good faith it became obvious that China placed very little value on India's goodwill. Mr. Nehru was curtly informed by Peking that it was not possible for him to visit Lhasa as had been anticipated, and added insult to injury by giving no reason for the refusal.

Although as much official silence as possible on the refusal to visit Lhasa was observed, the cavalier treatment by China rankled in Delhi. In a quicker diplomatic riposte than was usual with him, Mr. Nehru announced that he would continue with his intended visit to Bhutan. He had earlier been invited by the Government of Bhutan to visit Bhutan on his return from Lhasa, and his insistence on carrying out the visit was important for two reasons. One, he would still have to pass across fifteen miles of Tibetan territory, which made the Chinese specious excuse that the trip across Tibet was too dangerous look silly; and, two, it indicated a renewed interest on India's part on what was taking place in Tibet in relation to Bhutan in the light of India's treaty obligations to that country.

India had inherited her relations with Bhutan from the days of British rule, until she made a treaty of her own, the Indo-Bhutanese Treaty of 1949. This treaty read: 'The Government of India undertakes to exercise no interference in the internal affairs of Bhutan. On its part the Government of Bhutan agrees to be guided by the advice of the Government of India in regard to its external relations.' But in the intervening years since the signing of the Treaty there had been little interference or interest on the part of both countries. With seven thousand unpredictable Tibetan guerrillas and a militant Chinese army on Bhutan's borders it was time to do something.

When Mr. Nehru crossed from Sikkim into Tibet at the border-town of Yatung the Chinese made elaborate preparations to convey an impression of normality in that part of Tibet. Only a few soldiers were in evidence as a guard of honour to receive Mr. Nehru, but three thousand troops were stationed in the mountains surrounding the area to keep Tibetans from breaking through. Some rumours had been circulating that the Khambas intended kidnapping Mr. Nehru in order to have their predicament publicized and in order that he might be shown for himself what were the conditions.

The Chinese tried to get some of the leading Tibetan officials to meet Mr. Nehru to tell him that everything in Tibet was normal and that any other news he might have heard was only rumours emanating from Kalimpong, but they refused. A guerrilla representative, a former Khamba trader called Thosum, was deputed to present a statement and appeal to Mr. Nehru, but he was detected by the Chinese officials before he could do so and he had to escape to the mountains and through Bhutan into India.

Shortly after Mr. Nehru returned from Bhutan the road between Lhasa and Yatung became no longer usable by the Chinese as more and more groups of marauding Khamba guerrillas laid booby traps, attacked convoys and mowed down Chinese patrols.

The revolt in Tibet had at last reached the western borders, two thousand miles of them contiguous with India. To make matters more ominous a Soviet monthly journal, *The New Times*, followed up the Chinese publication, *New China*, with maps showing Ladakh, Kashmir, and the North-East Frontier area as belonging to China.

CHAPTER 17

Flight of the Dalai Lama

―――――

For a matter so gravely involving her frontier security India—
or, rather, Mr. Nehru, for other Indian leaders were not so com-
plaisant as he—was strangely reluctant to take any concrete action
to safeguard her own interests. In the matter of the maps Mr.
Nehru, in the Lok Sabha, said: 'So far as the Russian maps are
concerned I think they had merely copied them from the Chinese
maps without probably going into the matter. When we addressed
them they said that they would look into the matter. So far
as the Chinese maps are concerned we are still in correspondence.
As I have previously said their answer has been that these are old
maps—"we are not sure of the exact border and we shall look into
it and till then the *status quo* should continue".'

It was not just *laissez-faire*, but it seemed to stem from an attitude of complete uninterest in what was happening in Tibet, or
from a deliberate decision not to say or do anything that might
displease China.

There was no official reply to any of the appeals for help from
the Tibetans, and the unofficial communication was that the
Tibetans should not take part in armed revolt but should stage
non-violent demonstrations and civil disobedience campaigns
against the Chinese in Tibet.

Inside Tibet an ominous calm had settled over Lhasa and some
of the fighting areas following on the appeal to the United
Nations. The Chinese authorities made a final attempt to get the
Dalai Lama and the Lhasa Government to dissociate themselves
from the Appeal issued from Kalimpong, but were unsuccessful.
In the face of this defiance the Chinese then warned the Lhasa

officials that if they joined in the revolt the People's Liberation Army, thirty thousand strong in Lhasa, would bomb the city, including the Potala, the Dalai Lama's palace.

For the next few months there was no social or official contact between the Chinese and Tibetan officials at all. The Chinese, in a crude psychological attempt to bludgeon the Dalai Lama into submission, kept up a steady stream of Chinese official visitors to the Dalai Lama with demands that he declare the revolt a 'tribal affair', dissociate the Government from it and send the Tibetan Army against the rebels. The Dalai Lama resisted the pressure, still seeking to bargain for a peaceful solution to the Tibetan tragedy. But as it became more and more obvious that the Chinese had no intention of bargaining, a few trusted members of the Kashag began to make plans to leave the city.

Two groups of rebels were within forty miles of Lhasa, one to the north-east, and the other, the largest, to the south. The rebel group to the south had had several striking successes against the Chinese, and had captured an area of almost ten thousand square miles. With fifty-five 'dzongs', or district administrations, under their control they had their armed force of twenty thousand guerrillas and several hundred thousand civilians well organized. In order that they might not be infiltrated by Chinese spies, or paid Tibetan quislings, they had created a simple but well-organized administration to issue passports, collect taxes, ration food, requisition animals and generally carry out all the tasks necessary in guerrilla warfare over a vast area.

In addition to this area, they were also in touch with the Litang group of rebels, now in control of over ten thousand square miles in Kham and able to move through the widely-spaced Chinese lines separating them.

In December 1958 the Chinese authorities decided to try to break the impasse by removing the Dalai Lama to China. Probably the apparent success of their threat to bomb Lhasa if the people there revolted caused them to suppose that if the Dalai Lama were removed to China as a hostage, with the same threat against his life, the whole of Tibet would submit as had the people of Lhasa.

The Lhasa officials immediately countered by increasing the Dalai Lama's bodyguard from the usual five hundred to one thousand, and that in the teeth of Chinese disapproval. Also, units of the Tibetan Army of fifteen thousand, under trusted commanders, began manœuvres and rifle practice in the mountains when they could.

Three young Tibetans, two of them officials, Shudrun Lobsang Yeshi and Sampo Jigme, and one Manang Abu, a former wealthy Tibetan trader, relative of the Pangdatshang family, secretly began to recruit Lhasa civilians to join the rebels in the mountains south of Lhasa. Shudrun Lobsang Yeshi was a former monk official, favourite of the Regent Tagta Rimpoche, and after considerable indoctrination by the Communists he was considered one of the foremost Tibetan leaders among the young officials. It was this position which gave him the opportunity to cover his other patriotic activities in organizing the anti-Chinese Lhasa faction.

The Tibetan students who had been studying in Peking for the past five years formed anti-Communist organizations in both Lhasa and Peking. Nine sons of leading Tibetan families were arrested for this activity, one of them belonging to the Pangdatshang family, and the Chinese authorities refused the pleas of their mothers for their release until they had publicly confessed their errors. All nine remained obdurate.

In India the Indian Government moved to seal off completely any possible leakage of the situation in Tibet to the outside world. It had been obvious to me for some time that some sort of action would have to be taken against me, for having warned the Tibetan officials in India that they must not make statements to newspaper correspondents they could hardly leave me to go ahead and publicize the situation as I was doing.

In mid-February 1959 I was told by an official from the United Kingdom High Commission that the Indian Government had decided to take action against me for the articles I had been writing about the happenings in Tibet. There had been no specific allegation but the Ministry of External Affairs had claimed that I was guilty of sending misleading and exaggerated reports. He had not been asked officially to come to see me, but in view of the gravity of the action to be taken against me—and I ought to bear in mind that it was Mr. Nehru himself, and the head of the External Affairs Ministry, who had taken the decision—involving as it did the unprecedented dismissal of a British subject in India, he wanted to warn me and ask me to submit to the Indian Government's demand that I discontinue sending such reports.

I refused to agree, even after two hours' persuasion. I had thought over the matter, with all its possible implications, for several months, and was prepared to take the consequences. My reports were as factual as possible, short of witnessing the actual events, and I was prepared to stake my reputation on their veracity.

I agreed that it was obvious that India would not help, and would not permit others to give military help. I agreed that it was obvious that no pressure could be brought to bear on China to withdraw from Tibet. I agreed that it was obvious that the United Nations would stand aside as it had done in Hungary. But having said it all, I would not agree to sully my conscience by associating myself with any government which could connive not only at the murder of such a gallant nation but also at the deliberate intimidation of those who were that nation's only possible source of hope, if not help.

On February 28 I was ordered to attend the office of the local Deputy Commissioner and there I was told that 'unless he discontinued sending misleading and exaggerated messages about Tibet to the *Daily Telegraph* or other foreign papers, the Indian Government would be constrained to interdict his residence in the districts of Darjeeling, Jalapiguri and Cooch Behar'. I would be permitted, however, to send 'normal and objective' reports.

The official could give me no satisfactory explanation of what constituted a 'normal and objective' report, and what had been 'misleading and exaggerated' in my earlier articles. I had never been investigated as to my material or source at any time, and there was no specific allegation of misrepresentation in any of my writings. Accordingly, I told the official that I rejected the Government's demand, that I would continue sending reports as I received them until they took action against me, and that I refused to accept a verbal intimation in such an important matter and wanted the statement in writing so that I could take appropriate action.

The matter caused widespread controversy in press circles, both inside India and abroad. Mr. Nehru had to face questions at a press conference regarding his action against me and he there stated that press reports about revolts in Tibet 'were grossly exaggerated as a rule, for the simple reasons that the persons who give the news are refugees, who seldom are accurate witnesses—apart from being partisans who believe every rumour'. This was a remarkable statement from any point of view, for in addition to the fact that what I had written followed almost to the letter what he had been told by the Dalai Lama while in India and by the Dalai Lama's trusted Minister in a Memorandum to Mr. Nehru since, it also begged the obvious question as to where Mr. Nehru obtained his information if not from so-called 'refugees'. Certainly he could obtain very little through Indian Consulate channels in Lhasa, which were under strict Chinese observation. He had little contact except with Lhasa officials who were too scared to be seen with the Indian representative unless a Chinese official were there, and in any case he was considered too afraid of China to make worth while the risk of passing on information. Finally, the revolts were all outside Lhasa, several weeks' journey away in the mountains. Therefore Indian sources of information were also 'refugee' officials, traders, pilgrims—and partisans.

On March 17, in the Lok Sabha, the matter of my expulsion was again raised, and in reply Mr. Nehru said that 'the warning given recently to Mr. George Patterson is the kind of thing we do with reluctance'. Events in India were often misreported and misconstrued by foreign writers but they preferred to put up with criticism rather than interfere with the freedom of the press. They might have done the same in Mr. Patterson's case 'if we alone were concerned', but Mr. Patterson's reports had been so full of exaggeration that they had simply been compelled to warn him—'He accepted every bazaar rumour for a fact'. In his (Mr. Nehru's) opinion the situation in Tibet was 'a clash of minds rather than a clash of arms. I do not say that there is any large-scale violence there'.

Yet even as he was speaking revolt had broken out in Lhasa, and large-scale demonstrations had been going on in the city since March 10. On that day the Dalai Lama received an invitation from the Chinese authorities to attend a theatrical performance and tea at the Chinese military headquarters. This was an extraordinary occurrence for two reasons: one, the invitation was not conveyed through the Kashag as it should have been; and, two, the party was not at the palace where such functions would normally have been held, but at the military headquarters—and the Dalai Lama had been asked to attend alone.

A few days earlier there had been demonstrations when the Tibetans had gone to the Indian, Nepalese and Bhutanese Consulates to seek their help against the Chinese. When the report of the extraordinary invitation leaked out a crowd of over thirty thousand surrounded Norbulinka, the Dalai Lama's summer palace, and demonstrated against the Chinese action, refusing to let the Dalai Lama leave the palace to attend.

The demonstrations were kept up through the next day when five thousand women demonstrated in the streets and then presented an appeal to the Indian Consulate-General. The women were members of the Communist-inspired Patriotic Women's Association, ironically enough, and led by the wives of leading Tibetan officials, now incensed at the menace to the Dalai Lama.

The five-thousand-strong Tibetan Army billetted in Lhasa discarded their Chinese-supplied uniforms and announced their loyalty to the Dalai Lama.

In the face of this city-wide demonstration the Chinese authorities announced by loud-speaker that there had been a misunderstanding and that there was no intention of kidnapping the Dalai Lama. The Chinese version was that on March 10 General Tan Kuan-san, political commissar of the Area Command, wrote to the Dalai Lama suggesting that in view of the rumours by 'traitors' that a visit to a theatrical performance was a Chinese Communist pretext to detain him it would be better for him not to attend. According to Peking, the next day the Dalai Lama wrote:

'Reactionary, evil elements are carrying out activities endangering me under the pretext of protecting my safety. I am taking measures to calm things down.'

On the same day the General sent another letter in which he asked the local Tibetan Government to stop 'open military provocations':

'The reactionaries are now so audacious as to have openly and arrogantly carried out military provocations. They have erected fortifications and posted large numbers of machine-guns and armed reactionaries along the national defence highway (the highway north of the Norbulinka), thereby seriously disrupting the security of the national defence communications.

'Many times in the past we told the Kashag that the People's Liberation Army is in duty bound to defend the country and to protect the security of communication lines related to national defence, and therefore it certainly cannot remain indifferent to this serious act of military provocations. Therefore the Tibet Military Area Command has sent letters to Surkhang, Liusha, Shasu and Pala asking them to tell the reactionaries to remove all the fortifications they established and to withdraw from the highway immediately. Otherwise they will bear responsibility themselves for all the serious consequences. I want to inform you of this. Please let me know what your views are at your earliest convenience.'

The Dalai Lama replied:

'I have had the letter you sent me this morning. The unlawful actions of the reactionary clique break my heart. Yesterday I told the Kashag to order the immediate withdrawal of the reactionaries who arrogantly moved into the Norbulinka under the pretext of protecting me. As to the incidents of yesterday and the day before, which were created under the pretext of protecting my safety and have seriously estranged the relations between the Central Government and the Local Government, I am making every possible effort to deal with them. At 8.30 Peking time this morning a few Tibetan Army men suddenly fired several shots near the Chinghai-Tibet highway. Fortunately no serious disturbances occurred. As to the questions mentioned in your letter (referring to the letter of the 11th), I am planning to persuade my few subordinates and give them instructions. Please tell me frankly any instruction you have for me.'

On March 15 the tone of General Tan's correspondence became more peremptory:

'I have the honour to acknowledge receipt of your two letters dated March 11 and 12. The traitorous activities of the reactionary clique of the upper strata in Tibet have grown into intolerable proportions. These individuals, in collusion with foreigners, have engaged in reactionary, traitorous activities for some time. The Central People's Government has long adopted an attitude of magnanimity and enjoined the Local Government of Tibet to deal with them seriously, but the Local Government of Tibet has all along adopted an attitude of feigning compliance while actually helping their activities, with the result that things have now come to such a grave pass. The Central People's Government still hopes that the Local Government of Tibet will change its erroneous attitude and immediately assume responsibility for putting down the rebellion and mete out severe punishment to the traitors. Otherwise the Central People's Government will have to act itself to safeguard the solidarity and unification of the motherland. . . .

'We are very much concerned about your present position and safety. If you think it necessary and possible to extricate yourself from the present dangerous position of being abducted by the traitors, we cordially welcome you and your entourage to come and stay for a brief period in the Military Area Command. We are willing to assume full responsibility for your safety. . . .'

The Dalai Lama replied on the 16th:

'Your letter dated the 15th has just been received at 3 o'clock. I am very glad that you are so concerned for my safety, and hereby express my thanks.

'The day before yesterday, the fifth day of the Second Month according to the Tibetan calendar (March 14, 1959), I made a speech to more than seventy representatives of the Government officials, instructing them from various angles, calling on them to consider seriously present and long-term interests and to calm down, or my life would be in danger. After these severe reproaches, conditions took a slight turn for the better. Though the conditions in here and outside are still very difficult to deal with at present, I am trying skilfully to make a demarcation line between the progressive people and those opposing the revolution within the Government officials. A few days from now when there are enough forces that I can trust I shall make my way to the Military Area Command secretly. When that time comes, I shall first send you a letter. I request you to adopt reliable measures. What are your views? Please write me often.'

With the situation in the city, either directly or indirectly, beyond the control of the Dalai Lama and the Central People's Government, as may be seen from their correspondence, revolt was inevitable.

The chief figures behind the demonstrations were the three already mentioned, Shudrun Lobsang Yeshi, Sampo Jigme and Manang Abu. They had gathered over three thousand names of Lhasa Tibetans willing to join the rebel fighters in the mountains south of Lhasa. With this in mind Shudrun Lobsang Yeshi had been in contact with one of the Khamba leaders there.

Up to this time they had had no intention of staging an armed uprising in Lhasa, or of removing the Dalai Lama. But in the Kashag itself the Ministers were making plans to have the Dalai Lama removed to safety should the situation continue to deteriorate. Outside the Kashag only the chief of the Dalai Lama's bodyguard and the second-in-command knew what was being planned.

On March 15, following on General Tan's peremptory last letter, the decision to flee was taken.

At this point the plans of the three young Tibetans and the Kashag were co-ordinated. Three hundred of the Dalai Lama's bodyguard left on the 15th and stationed themselves quietly at two points, at Ramagang, eight miles from Norbulinka, on the River Kyi, and at Konka Dzong, thirty-five miles south of Lhasa on the south bank of the River Tsangpo. Shudrun Lobsang Yeshi arranged with Andrutshang, the Khamba rebel leader, to be at that point with another hundred and fifty Khambas of his own.

The second-in-command of the Dalai Lama's bodyguard, Sekshing, a minor noble, with the remaining two hundred of his men, was to remain behind with Manang Abu and Sampo Jigme. They would combine the Tibetan Army troops, equipped with machineguns and heavy artillery, and the civilian fighters, armed with ordinary rifles, into a force to cover the Dalai Lama's escape. Sampo Jigme was himself a battalion commander in the Tibetan Army, and his father was Commander-in-Chief.

There were reckoned to be between thirty thousand and fifty thousand Chinese troops in Lhasa, with seventeen heavy guns surrounding the city. In actual arms the Tibetans calculated that they were out-armed by about 100:4, and the Chinese guns were of superior and more modern quality. The Tibetan cannons in the fortifications in the city had to be wheeled into position by mules and were no match for the modern swivelling howitzers used by the Chinese.

On March 17, at 4 p.m., the Chinese troops fired several shells in the direction of the Norbulinka, all of them falling harmlessly into the muddy ground beside the pool in the Dalai Lama's summer palace.

No one knows why the Chinese chose to fire the shells then, unless they were supposed to serve as a warning to the Tibetans that the Chinese were ready to carry out their threat to bomb Lhasa and the Dalai Lama too, if necessary. Whatever the reason, the Dalai Lama accepted it as a threat against his person and decided that the time had come for him to flee.

It was an almost incredible venture, for the Chinese troops guarded every entrance and exit to and from the city. Chinese garrisons commanded strategic points to the north, south, east and west. Over thirty thousand Lhasa civilians still roamed the streets, and thousands had camped around the Norbulinka to ensure that no Chinese came near the Dalai Lama. The nearest guerrilla forces were forty miles away in the mountains to the south.

At 10 p.m. on March 17, dressed in ordinary lama clothes, the Dalai Lama walked unescorted out of the north gate of the Norbulinka, passed an armed Chinese garrison and made for Ramagang, eight miles away, where Shudrun Lobsang Yeshi had a boat ready at the ferry, with some members of the Dalai Lama's bodyguard, to take him down-river by night.

The party travelled through the night on the river for eight hours, finally landing at a point near Konka, where the River Kyi joined the River Tsangpo. Here the Khamba Leader, Andrutshang, with his Khamba guerrillas and the advance party of the Dalai Lama's bodyguard, were waiting. He was quickly escorted to Lhoka, Khamba-held territory in the mountains south of Lhasa, where he waited for the other members of his family and Kashag, coming by different escape routes.

Shudrun Lobsang Yeshi, having accomplished his part of the plan, returned up-river with some of his guerrilla fighters. He was met at Ramagang by a detachment of Chinese troops and in the fighting which followed, was killed.

Inside Norbulinka everything went on as usual, for only Sekshing had been told of the escape. The instructions to him and Sampo Jigme, his son-in-law, with Manang Abu, were to cover the escape as long as possible. They were so successful that the Dalai Lama's official photographer, Jigme Tering, living in the next room to Sekshing in the Norbulinka, did not know for three days that the Dalai Lama had gone.

Fighting began in Lhasa late in the night of March 19. Tibetans claim that the Chinese fired the first shot, which served as a signal for the whole city to join in, while the Chinese claim that the Tibetans launched an all-out attack on the Chinese garrisons on the night of the 19th and that it was only at 10 a.m. on March 20 that the troops of the Tibetan Military Area Command of the People's Liberation Army were ordered to take punitive action.

Fierce fighting continued in and around the city for two days. Eight hundred shells were poured on to the Norbulinka, destroying about three hundred houses belonging to leading officials and killing thousands of men, women and children surrounding the summer palace to 'protect' the Dalai Lama. The Chinese thought that the Dalai Lama was still in the Norbulinka and they tried to use the opportunity to kill him and rid themselves of their greatest obstacle at a time when they could blame the 'reactionaries' for staging the revolt and making the firing necessary.

That the Chinese knew nothing of the Dalai Lama's escape was obvious from their claim that he was 'under duress' of the 'upper-strata reactionaries and traitorous clique', thus making it easy for them to 'recover' him at an early date as they obviously expected. Also, they asked the Indian, Nepalese and Bhutanese Consulates in Lhasa for permission to search their premises for the Dalai Lama, indicating that they had no idea where he was, and even that they suspected the Indian, Nepalese and Bhutanese of 'kid-napping' him and keeping him on their premises.

It was ironical that on the same day that Mr. Nehru had de-clared that I was being expelled because my reports were mis-leading and exaggerated, and that what was happening in Tibet was not violence but a clash of minds rather than a clash of arms, the Dalai Lama made his escape. Two days later the Indian Prime Minister had to announce that the Indian Consulate had been hit in the fighting.

It was a hopeless battle from the start, and in the two days of merciless fighting the Chinese killed thousands of Tibetans. No figures are available but more than ten thousand Lhasa Tibetans are known to have disappeared, either killed or sent into forced labour in other parts.

The two hundred members of the Dalai Lama's bodyguard who had been left behind were disarmed, then publicly machine-gunned. The famous three large monasteries of Sera, Drepung and Ganden were shelled, and Sera and Drepung damaged be-yond repair, priceless manuscripts and treasures being destroyed. Thousands of monks from these monasteries were either killed on the spot, made to work in the city as slaves, or deported to other parts.

The Potala, the Dalai Lama's winter palace and seat, was hit by seventeen shells and the walls, at least, badly damaged.

When the fighting had died down the Chinese troops made a house-to-house search. They did not find many rebels; most of those who could had already fled to the mountains to join the Khamba rebels there, but in the houses where they found arms the residents and their families were taken out and shot on the spot.

In the meantime the Chinese News Agency in Peking was desperately trying to deny that there had been any revolt in Lhasa at all, and to claim that the Dalai Lama had been abducted 'under duress' by the Khamba guerrillas and would be recovered soon. Spotter planes covered the territory to the east between Lhasa and Sikkim and Lhasa and Nepal, which was the shortest and most likely route for the Dalai Lama to take if he were making for India.

CHAPTER 18

The Dalai Lama in India

In India furious controversy broke out in the press and in Parliament. Both institutions felt that either Mr. Nehru had been deliberately misleading them in his recent statements or that the Indian Government was seriously misinformed on what was actually happening inside Tibet.

Two days after the fighting in Lhasa, Mr. Nehru announced in the Indian Parliament that bullets had struck the Indian Consulate-General and the Chinese had ordered the staff to remain inside the Consulate until further notice. His voice was drowned in the shouting and turmoil which followed his statement. When order was restored he declined to allow the Tibetan situation to be discussed, or even the matter of the Indian Government's refusal to allow Tibetan refugees to enter India, as 'India has no intention of interfering in the internal affairs of China, with whom we have very friendly relations'. But for once Mr. Nehru had underestimated Indian feeling, and the matter continued to make headlines in India's newspapers. There were demonstrations against China's action in several cities.

Indian and world interest was sustained by the extraordinary escape of the Dalai Lama with his family and Government from the midst of two hundred thousand Chinese troops and the mounting drama of whether they could reach the border and safety across the most difficult terrain in the world.

Indian and foreign correspondents began pouring into the controversial border town of Kalimpong, looking for news of the revolt and the possible whereabouts of the Dalai Lama. From March 15 no Tibetans had come through on the Lhasa-Yatung

16. The Dalai Lama on his arrival, surrounded by Indian and Tibetan Government officials

17. The Dalai Lama in cheerful mood greeting the author (out of picture) at his Press Conference in Mussoorie, in June, 1959

18. Birla House, Mussoorie, the Dalai Lama's exile house in India

19. The platform party of Indian political leaders and the Tibetan representatives, Sonam Gyaltsho and Tethong Sey, at the open-air mass rally of the All-India Tibet Convention in Calcutta following on the violent suppression of the revolt in Tibet

highway so no up-to-date news was available, but it did not hinder a stream of speculation—and more bazaar rumours than I could pick up in ten years—making the headlines. For ten days after the last despatch giving news of the outbreak of the revolt in Lhasa there was not one iota of information available, and I sent no despatches, yet in those ten days Tibet was a front-page sensation inside and outside India.

On March 30 the Chinese authorities made their first statements, one from their Embassy in New Delhi, when they accused Luk-hangwa, the former Tibetan Prime Minister left behind by the Dalai Lama, as the leader of the rebels, and Kalimpong as the rebels' 'commanding centre', and the other from Peking radio giving an account of a cable received from the Panchen Lama reading: 'On behalf of the Tibetan people, ecclesiastical and secular, and in my name, I hail the tremendous victory already won by the People's Liberation Army in putting down the rebellion'.

A delegation of leading Tibetan officials in India, led by Luk-hangwa, went to New Delhi, and after presenting Mr. Nehru with the traditional offering of scarves handed over another Memorandum. In addition to asking help for the Dalai Lama the Memorandum urged:

'Red Cross assistance for Tibetans wounded in the recent fighting in Lhasa.

'Indian sponsorship for a Tibetan demand already before the United Nations for freedom from the Chinese Communists.

'Permission for refugees to cross the frontier into India.'

No one knew the route of the Dalai Lama's escape, but by close questioning of those Tibetans who were *au fait* with the events leading up to the revolt I deduced that he was making for the Indian border at Assam. This included a wide area, but I was helped in my deduction by knowing the details of the Dalai Lama's brother's escape route from Lhasa in 1952 and guessed that the Dalai Lama was following the same trail.

With a score of correspondents in Kalimpong, and others gathering in Shillong, in Assam, I chartered a plane belonging to the Indian Tea Association and made for Tezpur, in Upper Assam, the nearest point in Indian territory at which the Dalai

Lama would emerge. The reason for my secrecy and desire to meet the Dalai Lama before the other correspondents was not primarily to 'scoop' the story, but because I was convinced that once the Dalai Lama arrived in India he would be ordered to keep quiet by the Indian Government and would have no opportunity to make his and his country's predicament known. It was imperative, therefore, that I meet him before he was officially met and warned to keep quiet on Indian soil.

I had cabled the head office of the *Daily Telegraph* to put me in touch with another correspondent who could cover the situation, without revealing my plans to disappear for a few days in search of the Dalai Lama, for my mail was being opened. The head office cabled me that they were sending John Osman to help. When I slipped away to Tezpur I left word with my wife to tell John Osman to follow me there.

The route which I expected the Dalai Lama to take ran almost in a straight line through South Tibet and reached the Indian border at the Tibetan frontier post of Tsona Dzong. Leaving Tsona Dzong he would be in Indian territory in a matter of hours but still several days within the Inner Defence Line of the North-East Frontier Area forbidden to everyone, foreigners and Indian nationals alike. This Inner Defence Line was about forty miles north of the small town of Tezpur in North Assam.

I had friends amongst the tea-planting community there, and it was my intention to go there, make what arrangements I could regarding supplies, then with my Tibetan servant to slip across the frontier at night on the five-day mountain journey to meet the Dalai Lama at a point on his route through the North-East Frontier Area before he arrived in India. The penalty if we were caught was five years' imprisonment.

While I was still getting together supplies for the trip John Osman, my colleague on the *Daily Telegraph*, arrived, accompanied by two other correspondents, Noel Barber of the *Daily Mail* and Bertram Jones of the *Daily Express*. This was an unexpected complication, for where two people had a slight chance of crossing the forbidden area unseen five people had very little chance.

However, all were prepared to risk it, and at nine o'clock that night we slipped away by car to a point near the border where I had arranged for guides to take us through the ten miles of jungle before reaching the mountains. On the way the headlights of the car picked out the gleaming eyes and form of a tiger disappearing into the jungle beside the road.

Apparently this was nothing, for when we arrived at our rendezvous and the guides found out that it was our intention to go through the jungle unarmed, and even without torches, they flatly refused to go. They claimed that not only were there tigers but herds of wild elephants as well, and in addition the units of the Assam Rifles would shoot at sight anything or anyone moving at night. We put up the price to £10 each for a guide to take us one night through the jungle, but on the pretext that they were going outside to discuss it they slipped away into the darkness and nothing more was seen of them. The trip had to be called off, for without guides a night journey through the jungle was impossible.

Next day, when it became known that several leading correspondents were making it their headquarters, Tezpur began to fill up with journalists from all over the world. There was no hotel accommodation, and the Tezpur Planters' Club had no facilities for boarding people, so famous correspondents were sleeping on couches, billiard tables and wherever they could put up. The planters, who rarely ever saw visitors in their remote plantations, hospitably put up two, three and four correspondents, and Ronnie and Mary de la Rue Browne, where I was staying, put up five without complaint.

Tezpur's two ancient taxis had been requisitioned by the first arrivals so that no others could take them over, and were being held night and day at a hire of two rupees an hour plus petrol, whether used or not. Private planes were also chartered for anything up to a fortnight and even longer, depending on the guess of the particular correspondent as to when the Dalai Lama would arrive.

As newspaper correspondent rivals gathered so the attempts at 'scoops' multiplied, and incidents involving two world famous newspapers and two world famous news agencies indicate how high was the tension.

A famous correspondent had anticipated a scoop by chartering a plane to fly over the Dalai Lama's party travelling through the North-East Frontier Area, and had sent off his imaginative report before leaving Calcutta for Assam. In the plane he told this to the other correspondents travelling with him, and gloated over the fact that there was nothing they could do about it now for by the time the plane landed at Tezpur it would be too late for them to get an article into that night's paper, and next day he would fly over the North-East Frontier Area, take some photographs and thus complete his scoop. But when they checked with the pilot they discovered that it was forbidden to fly over the frontier territory, no pilot would touch it, and the correspondent was left with an article which he couldn't kill in time—and the possibility of five years in gaol for something he did not do. When a few days later an equally famous rival arrived in Tezpur, also with a chartered plane, he was convinced that his rival was going to make the attempt and he frantically sought a pilot who would take the risk, even offering up to £1,000. Both were unsuccessful, but I found a pilot who was willing to go, passed the word on to John Osman, as I was not in the position to use the opportunity, and he and the other correspondent finally made the flight after all—but in the altered circumstances neither could use it and they were left only with the photographs to prove their flight.

The other incident happened after the Dalai Lama had arrived in India. Almost two hundred correspondents were clamouring for news. The border was completely sealed, the usual press facilities were absent, there were near-farcical security arrangements with correspondents being followed everywhere, the tea planters had been warned not to assist the press, officials were completely silent even on innocuous items of information, and no one knew when the Dalai Lama would arrive—or even if he was coming that way at all, for it was still only a matter of guesswork. The press had to resort to books, geographical and even anthropological, to keep the story alive.

When it was known that the Dalai Lama was coming and would

arrive at Tezpur on April 18, leaving again that same day at 12.50 p.m., the authorities stated that no one would be allowed to leave the small Tezpur airfield (which nine chartered planes were using) until after he had gone at 1 p.m. In the rush to get away first the United Press Agency was successful, and its famous rival, the Associated Press Agency, immediately followed. In the air the pilots of the two planes sought to confuse each other by radioing wrong locations in their race for Calcutta with their exclusive photographs. United Press got there first, and on arrival at the Central Telegraph Office put in seven photographs—each taking twenty minutes to radio—so that Associated Press could not get in for two hours, when their photographs would be of little use. It was a major scoop all right—or would have been if something had not gone wrong.

Somehow Associated Press managed to slip a photograph into the radioing process, so that after the first two United Press photographs had been sent there was inserted an Associated Press photograph, then the remaining five belonging to the United Press. Shortly afterwards a frantic cable from the United Press head office was received: 'Your Dalai Lama not Associated Press Dalai Lama stop Check.'

The United Press correspondent replied: 'My Dalai Lama right Dalai Lama.'

Back came another cable from the United Press head office: 'Your Dalai Lama has hair stop Check.'

And sorrowfully the correspondent had to reply: 'Kill my Dalai Lama stop Mistake.'

He had taken photographs of the interpreter instead of the Dalai Lama.

But while the press fought for scraps of information on the India border of Tibet an ominous situation was building up in the Communist Government-controlled press in China.

After announcing—to the consternation of the Indian Government, which, as I have said, had gone to farcical lengths to prevent any leakage of information as to the Dalai Lama's whereabouts—that they had news that the Dalai Lama and his party, including members of his family and Government, had crossed into India on

The Dalai Lama in India

March 31, Mr. Nehru reluctantly admitted to the Government two days later that this was the case. How the Chinese had come to find out was a matter of grave concern, some suggesting that it indicated the Chinese were in possession of India's secret code.

Giving a full account of the revolt for the first time, the New China News Agency said that Chang Kuo-hua, Vice-Chairman of Tibet's Preparatory Committee, had assumed the powers of Local Government under the Panchen Lama. The Tibetan rebels in the recent revolt in Lhasa had been 'closely linked with rebels in Sikang' (the Chinese name for Kham). Chang claimed that the proof of this link was 'the large quantity of materials acquired during the course of putting down the rebellion'. A rough count showed that by March 23 more than four thousand rebel troops were taken prisoner and that eight thousand small arms of various kinds, eighty-one light and heavy machine-guns, twenty-seven eighty-one-millimetre calibre mortars, six mountain guns and ten million bullets had been captured. The rebels were given access to ammunition, food and other materials by the Local Government, and a number of officials, members of the Tibetan Army and lamas from the monasteries, went over to the rebels with arms issued by the Government.

The attack against India mounted until it became a nation-wide affair, with public denunciation meetings all over the country. The gravamen of their accusations was that 'Indian expansionists and British imperialists have not given up their ambition to invade Tibet and enslave its people'. The centre for this supposedly subversive group was alleged to be Kalimpong, 'the commanding centre of the revolt', where British imperialists (represented by myself), Indian expansionists (represented by Jayaprakash Narayan, Acharya Kripalani, Apa Sahib B. Pant, the Political Officer in Sikkim, and others) and leading Tibetan officials in India were supposed to have connived in their activities. 'During the past eight years, under the support of imperialism—particularly that of the British imperialists and Indian expansionists—the traitorous clique headed by Lukhangwa, Surkhang Wongchen, Shudrun Lobsang Yeshi, Pala Thubden, Liusha Thupten-Tarpa, Shakabpa, Gyalu Thondup, Yuthok and Kundeling Tzasa, have conducted a series of traitorous and subversive activities.' They then went on to describe how I had laid the groundwork of the revolt in Kham from 1947–50, and then with my contacts through the Pangdat-shangs, both Rapga and Yangpel, and other Lhasa Government officials listed above, organized the revolt which had just taken place.

In the Indian Parliament Mr. Nehru denied that Kalimpong was the centre of the revolt, 'but I have said it was a centre of trouble. It has been described as a "nest of spies", of innumerable nationalities—spies from Asia, spies from America, Communist spies, white spies, red spies, blue spies and pink spies.'

The unbridled attack on India only served to increase Indian sympathy for Tibet and press and public were both in full support of help for the Dalai Lama and any Tibetans who might require it. The volume of sympathy was so great that even Mr. Nehru had to bow before it, and after having said that India would receive no Tibetan refugees he reversed his decision and agreed to reconsider the question when the refugees presented themselves on India's borders. It was the same with the Tibetan situation. Having said that it could not be discussed in Parliament, and showing every reluctance to commit himself to any statement, he finally agreed under pressure to a date for the discussion of the problem.

This reluctance on the part of India's Prime Minister to displease China augured ill for Tibet. For Mr. Nehru was India in the councils of the world, and if he was not prepared to speak or to help then no other country could come to the help of Tibet, whatever form the contemplated aid might take.

On April 18 the Dalai Lama, his mother, sister, one brother, three ministers and about eighty others arrived at Tezpur. He was closely guarded by police, and the press were not allowed to interview him. But a statement was issued by him and read by an interpreter on his behalf, the full text of which was as follows:

'It has always been accepted that the Tibetan people are different from the Han people of China. There has always been a strong desire for independence on the part of the Tibetan people. Throughout history this has been asserted on numerous occasions.

'Sometimes the Chinese Government have imposed their suzerainty on Tibet, and at other times Tibet has functioned as an independent country. In any event, at all times, even when the suzerainty of China was imposed, Tibet remained autonomous in control of its internal affairs.

'In 1951, under pressure of the Chinese Government, a Seventeen-point Agreement was made between China and Tibet. In that Agreement the suzerainty of China was accepted as there was no alternative left to the Tibetans. But even in that Agreement it was stated that Tibet would enjoy full autonomy. Though the control of external events was to be in the hands of the Chinese Government, it was agreed that there would be no interference by the Chinese Government with the Tibetan religion and customs and her internal administration. In fact, after the occupation of Tibet by the Chinese armies, the Tibetan Government did not enjoy any autonomy, even in internal matters, and the Chinese Government exercised full powers in Tibetan affairs.

'In 1956 a Preparatory Committee was set up for Tibet with the Dalai Lama as Chairman and the Panchen Lama as Vice-Chairman, and General Chang Kuo-hua as the representative of the Chinese Government. In practice even this body had little power and decisions in all important matters were taken by the Chinese authorities.

'The Dalai Lama and his Government tried their best to adhere to the Seventeen-point Agreement, but the interference of the Chinese authorities persisted.

'By the end of 1955 a struggle had started in the Kham Province and this assumed serious proportions in 1956. In the consequential struggle the Chinese armed forces destroyed a large number of monasteries. Many lamas were killed and a large number of monks and officials were employed on the construction of roads in China, and the interference in the exercise of religious freedom increased. The relations of Tibetans with China became openly strained from the early part of February 1959.

'The Dalai Lama had agreed a month in advance to attend a cultural show in the Chinese headquarters and the date was suddenly fixed for March 10. The people of Lhasa became apprehensive that some harm might be done to the Dalai Lama. As a result about ten thousand people gathered around the Dalai Lama's summer palace in Norbulinka and physically prevented the Dalai Lama from attending the function. Thereafter the people themselves decided to raise a bodyguard for the protection of the Dalai Lama. Large crowds of Tibetans went about the streets of Lhasa demonstrating against the Chinese rule in Tibet. Two days later thousands of Tibetan women held demonstrations protesting against the Chinese authority.

'In spite of this demonstration from the people, the Dalai Lama and his Government endeavoured to maintain friendly relations with the Chinese and tried to carry out negotiations with the Chinese representatives as to how best to bring about peace in Tibet and assuage the people's anxiety.

'While these negotiations were being carried out reinforcements arrived to strengthen the Chinese garrisons in Lhasa and Tibet. On March 17 two or three mortar shells were fired in the direction of the Norbulinka Palace. Fortunately the shells fell in a nearby pond. After this the advisers became alive to the danger to the person of the Dalai Lama and in those difficult circumstances it became imperative for the Dalai Lama, the members of his family and his high officials to leave Lhasa.

'The Dalai Lama would like to state categorically that he left Lhasa and Tibet and came to India of his own free will and not under duress. It was due to the loyalty and affectionate support of his people that the Dalai Lama was able to find his way through a route which is quite arduous.

'The route which the Dalai Lama took involved crossing the River Kyi and the River Tsangpo (Brahmaputra) and making his way through the Lhoka area, Yarlung Valley and Tsona Dzong before reaching the Indian frontier at Kanzey Mane, near Chutangmu. On March 29 the Dalai Lama sent two emissaries to cross the Indo-Tibetan border requesting the Government of India's permission to enter India and seek asylum there.

'The Dalai Lama is extremely grateful to the people and Government of India for their spontaneous and generous welcome, as well as the asylum granted to him and his followers. India and

The Dalai Lama in India

Tibet have had religious, cultural and trade links for over a thousand years and for Tibet it has always been the land of enlightenment, having given birth to the Lord Buddha. The Dalai Lama is deeply touched by the kind greetings extended to him on his safe arrival in India by the Prime Minister, Mr. Nehru, and his colleagues in the Government of India. The Dalai Lama has already sent a reply to this message of greetings.

'Ever since the Dalai Lama entered India at Kanzey Mane, near Chutangmu, he has experienced in full measure the respect and hospitality extended to him by the people of the Kameng frontier division of the North-East Frontier Agency. The Dalai Lama would like to state how the Government of India's officers posted there had spared no effort in making his stay and journey through the extremely well-administered part of India as comfortable as possible.

'The Dalai Lama will now be proceeding to Mussoorie, which he hopes to reach in the next few days. The Dalai Lama will give thought to his future plans and if necessary give expression to them as soon as he has had a chance to rest and reflect on recent events. His country and people have passed through an extremely difficult period and all that the Dalai Lama wishes to say at the moment is to express his sincere regret at the tragedy which has overtaken Tibet and to hope fervently that these troubles will be over soon without any more bloodshed.

'As Dalai Lama and spiritual head of all Buddhists in Tibet his foremost concern is the well-being of his people and in ensuring the perpetual flourishing of his sacred religion and the freedom of his country.

'While expressing once again thankfulness at his safe arrival in India, the Dalai Lama would like to take this opportunity to communicate to all his friends, well-wishers and devotees in India and abroad his sincere gratitude for many messages of sympathy and concern with which they have flooded him.'

But it was at Siliguri, the railhead junction for Kalimpong and Darjeeling, on his way to Mussoorie, that he met the largest concentration of Tibetans in India. Seven thousand Tibetans from Kalimpong, Darjeeling and Sikkim had gathered to see the

The Dalai Lama in India

Dalai Lama during the period of the train's one-hour scheduled stop.

Here again security arrangements reached the farcical stage, and only members of the Dalai Lama's family living in India, the Sikkim and Bhutan royal families, with certain Indian officials, were allowed near the Dalai Lama. The press were kept behind a roped enclosure, and hundreds of extra police were drafted in to keep people at a safe distance. Even the exiled cabinet ministers and other leading Tibetan officials from Kalimpong were not allowed near the station platform, and when they tried to approach were rudely shouted at by a police official from twenty yards away to 'Get away from here', and were hustled away like obstreperous coolies to a platform a hundred yards distant. The Government obviously wanted to keep the situation in Tibet from getting undue publicity and thus forcing them into taking some sort of stand before world opinion. When an official tried to remonstrate quietly with the Inspector-General of Police who was shouting at and driving the Tibetan officials away, the Inspector-General shrugged him off and shouted at him, 'I have my orders!'

However, the press, discouraged and faint but still pursuing, continued to Mussoorie, the hill station in North India where a house had been made ready for the Dalai Lama and his party. There Mr. Nehru had arranged to meet the Dalai Lama for the first time since his arrival in India. The press were permitted fifteen minutes for photographs of the momentous meeting, but no interviews with the Dalai Lama.

Mr. Nehru spent four hours with the Dalai Lama, and had two meetings with the press, one before and one after his talk with the Dalai Lama. He was cordial but cautious. He said that the Dalai Lama was tired after his recent escape and journey and wanted nothing more than rest for some time. They had discussed the Tibetan situation, but nothing concrete had been suggested by either of them, and both hoped for an early and peaceful solution.

Most of the correspondents left Mussoorie after this, but a few, among them Heinrich Harrer of *Seven Years in Tibet* fame and myself, stayed on, still hopeful of a private interview or a more

187

specific statement of some kind from the Dalai Lama. But we might have saved ourselves the trouble.

The Indian authorities were determined that no one would get near the Dalai Lama or his party to obtain details of what had happened and was likely to happen in Tibet. Security arrangements went beyond the merely exasperating to the ludicrous. Even the fiction which some officials sought to propagate that strict security had to be maintained so that no harm might come to the Dalai Lama in India ceased to have significance when the tall, powerful Khambas, who guarded the Dalai Lama safely from Lhasa to India, had to be escorted by two scrawny plainclothes policemen when they made purchases in the bazaar in Mussoorie.

Those who, like Harrer and myself, spoke Tibetan and were friendly with several people in the Dalai Lama's party, were even more closely watched. There were two security police to every correspondent, but Harrer and I had seven to keep us covered. The hotel reception clerk was instructed to listen to every conversation, check on all telephone calls and find out whom we visited and when. Even an American photographer, whose assignment was the open and innocent one of trying to persuade any of the Dalai Lama's party to sell him photographs of their journey, found that his private mail was being carelessly opened and even more carelessly closed. Behind barbed wire fencing, armed guards patrolled and floodlights kept the night like day. One correspondent had the perilous indignity of having a gun pointed at him and the safety catch released when he wandered too near the fence in daylight. The Dalai Lama's young brother was escorted through the bazaar by the chief security officer himself, and even each servant had a security policeman escorting him whenever he ventured out. Kalimpong exile officials who arrived for talks with the Dalai Lama were warned that if they 'leaked' any information they would also be confined to Birla House, and they were so intimidated that they would not allow their servants, or even their sons, into the room with them when they talked with others—an unprecedented occurrence in a Tibetan household. The conclusion was obvious: the Indian Government was not so much worried over the security of the Dalai Lama as about what some member of his party might say concerning the situation in Tibet.

It might be doing the Indian Government an injustice to come to this conclusion, for the decision primarily lay with Mr. Nehru and one or two associates. Many members of the Government, and many members of his Congress Party, strongly objected to the way Mr. Nehru was handling the Tibetan situation, but there was little they could do about it. Press sympathy and public sentiment had already carried an obviously reluctant Mr. Nehru far beyond the point he personally wished to go, and he seemed determined to do as little as he possibly need.

In Calcutta an All Indian Tibet Convention was called to protest against China's action in Tibet and to discuss ways and means of helping the Tibetans. At first Mr. Nehru's Congress Party participated enthusiastically, but a few days before the Convention was held the Congress Party in West Bengal received a directive from the Delhi headquarters ordering them, without any explanation, to withdraw. In his presidential address, Jayaprakash Narayan, the famous Indian Socialist leader who is spoken of as Nehru's successor, strongly deplored the Government's past and present actions over Tibet. Mr. Nehru should lead Indian and world opinion in condemning aggression in Tibet, he maintained. No attempt should be made for reasons of diplomacy to play down, cover up, belittle or misrepresent what was happening in Tibet.

'The policy of Chinese suzerainty over Tibet was born in imperialist sin and the Indian Government is condoning it. India's acceptance of the suzerainty formula has given the Chinese moral and legal sanction and prevented the formulation of an Afro-Asian opinion on Tibet.

'It has prevented the true aggressive character of Chinese Communism from being realized by the backward people of Asia, aggravating the danger of their being enslaved in the name of liberation.'

Acharya Kripalanai, Leader of the Opposition in the Indian Parliament, went even further. In answer to a question regarding his opinion of China's intentions he stated that China's intentions were the same as Russia's: to nibble away at countries on the border, slowly absorbing them in a policy of expansion. Now that China had taken over Tibet her next move would be into Bhutan, Sikkim or Nepal.

On June 20, 1959, the Dalai Lama called a Press Conference at Mussoorie. To a hundred and thirty press correspondents, representing newspapers from all over the world, he answered ninety-two questions from fourteen different sources. He was outspoken on Chinese actions in Tibet, commiserated with the Panchen Lama in what he claimed were enforced statements and activities, expressed his gratitude to India for her help until now, and appealed to the world to take some action to help Tibet. He stated that the ultimate Chinese aim in Tibet was 'an attempted domination of the Tibetan religion and culture, and absorption of the Tibetan race'. Giving a brief account of events in Lhasa since the revolt and his escape he said that the people of Lhasa had been divided into three groups. The first group was deported to China, where their fate was not known. The second group was imprisoned, interrogated and punished without limit in the various Chinese military headquarters in and around Lhasa. The third group was committed to forced labour and given a minimum amount of food for a maximum amount of labour. Mass killings of clergy and laity were taking place, and over one thousand monasteries had already been destroyed and gutted of all treasures. Instead of respecting his office as they had solemnly agreed to do the Chinese had persistently worked at undermining his authority and creating dissensions amongst the Tibetans. Even in 1956 things had reached such a state that he had made up his mind not to return to Tibet had it not been for the assurances and persuasions of Mr. Nehru.

These promises were not fulfilled. Instead, the Chinese tyrannies increased until it became impossible for him and the Tibetan Government to control any longer the spontaneous upsurge of the Tibetan people in revolt against the Chinese oppressors.

The Dalai Lama ended his statement to the representatives of the world's press with an appeal for their interest and help in Tibet's struggle for freedom, and even existence.

The Dalai Lama in India

'To you gentlemen of the press I and my people owe a great debt of gratitude for all that you have done to assist us in our struggle for survival and freedom. Your sympathy and support have given us courage and strengthened our determination. I confidently hope that you will continue to lend that weight of your influence to the cause of peace and freedom for which the people of Tibet are fighting today.'

This same expression of gratitude he reiterated to me during a private interview which I had with him on August 20, 1959:

'I have heard many things concerning Khamba Gyau ("The Bearded Khamba", my Tibetan name) and the great help you have been to Tibet. But even more than in the past you must help us now, in whatever way you can.'

I can do no more than finish this further contribution towards the help of Tibet, meagre and futile as it seems, than by quoting the statement made in the Introduction to the Preliminary Report of the International Commission of Jurists on 'The Question of Tibet and the Rule of Law':

'The danger in such cases as that of Tibet is of a feeling of impotence and powerlessness overcoming people in the face of a *fait accompli*—a mixture of indifference, lack of moral courage and determination. . . . What happened in Tibet yesterday may happen in our own countries tomorrow. The force of public opinion, however, cannot be disregarded; ideas will penetrate where bullets will not.'

Index

Index

Index

Manchus, 24, 25; revolt of East Tibet against, 39
Mao Tse-tung, 67, 126
Markham, 39, 53, 152
Ma Su, 51
Mekong, R., 38
Menon, Krishna, 67, 77, 94
Mi-mang-Tsong-du (People's Party against Communist China), 90, 106, 109, 112–14, 119, 131
Mineral resources of Tibet, 122
Minya Konka Mountains, 33, 34
Monasteries, destruction of, 127, 149–50, 174, 184, 190
Mongols, 37; and Sixth Dalai Lama, 23, 24; stationed troops in Tibet, 25
Moscow, 95
Mussoorie, 186

Nagchuka Province, 53
Nankin, 53
Narayan, Jayaprakash, 160; deplores Indian Government's Tibetan policy, 189
Nehru, Mr., and border states, 95, 103, 109, 136; meets Dalai Lama and Chou En-lai, 138–9; proposes to visit Tibet, 149; challenged on concept of Panch Shila, 160; visit to Tibet vetoed by China, 161; visits Bhutan, 161; shows reluctance to intervene, 161, 163, 165–8; proposes expulsion of G.P., 166 seqq.; meets Dalai Lama in Mussoorie, 187
Nepal, and Britain, 27; and Communist threat, 63, 95 seqq., 103, 175
New China (Chinese journal), 162, 182
New Delhi, 53, 60, 102; Tibetan Trade Mission to, 60; Tibetan delegation to after Dalai Lama's escape, 177
New Times, The (Soviet journal), 162
New York Times, 96
Ngabu, 65 seqq., 68, 74, 75
Norbulinka, the, 168, 169, 172, 173, 185
North-East Frontier areas, 162, 178
Nyarong, 26

Opium War, 26
Osman, John, 178, 180

Pakistan, 95
Panchen Lama, creation of office, 21; proposed as regent by Imperial Government, 29; as Chinese puppet, 53, 177; supports Communist 'liberation' of Tibet, 67; enters Lhasa with Chinese troops, 85, 109; used by Communists to divide Tibetan loyalties, 107–9; visits China with Dalai Lama, 108; visits India, 137 seqq.; assumes power in Tibetan Government after Dalai Lama's escape, 182
Panch Shila (Five Principles), 103, 119, 138, 160
Pangdatshang, Topgyay, 52–3, 65, 74; created Colonel by Chiang Kai-shek' 56; military leader of Khambas against Chinese Communists, 64
Pangdatshang, Rapga, 52–3, 57, 64, 65, 74; and Democratic Reform Party, 57; expelled by British from Kalimpong to China, 58; moderate policy of, 58; plan to form new Representative Government for Greater Tibet, 66; Governor of Markham, 1953, in India, 1955, 117 seqq.; disillusionment with America, 126; refuses to support Chul-ka Sum, 153
Pangdatshang, Yangpel, 57, 74, 77
Pannikar, Sardar K. M., 64, 75, 77
Patel, Sirdar, 76
Peking, 25, 67, 95
People's Liberation Army, 78, 80, 85, 86, 88, 105, 144, 169
People's Political Consultative Committee, 100, 134
Potala, the, 22
Preparatory Committee for the Autonomous Region of Tibet, 108, 110. 118, 133, 157, 184

Radhakrishnan, Dr. 137
Ramagan, 171, 173
Regionalism in Tibet, 32–5, 42
Reting Hutukhtu, 53, 74, appointed Regent, 52; and discovery of Fourteenth Dalai Lama, 54; murdered by Tagta, 56
Road building, 86, 99, 100
Russia, 77–8, 95

Sadiya, 58
Sakya lamas, 19
Salween River, 38
Sampo Jigme, 165, 171 seqq.
San Min Chu-i or Three Principles of the People (Sun Yat Sen), 57
Sera monastery, 84, 174
Serpent Gods, temple to, 22
Seventeen-Point Agreement, 68, 78, 82, 96, 112, 144, 156, 184
Seven Years in Tibet, Harrer, 73, 187
Shakabpa (Finance Secretary), 60, 67, 73, 74, 116
Shamanism, 36
Shambala, 74
Shensi Province, 18
Shigatse, Gurkha capture of, 25

Index